Sallie J Hancock

Rayon D'Amour

Poems

Sallie J Hancock

Rayon D'Amour
Poems

ISBN/EAN: 9783744710640

Printed in Europe, USA, Canada, Australia, Japan

Cover: Foto ©Thomas Meinert / pixelio.de

More available books at **www.hansebooks.com**

Rayon d'Amour.

POEMS.

BY

SALLIE J. HANCOCK.

AUTHOR OF THE MONTANAS.

"Via Crucis — via Lucis."

"Long had he been a thing of common clay,
A being of earthly mould:
But lo! an angel crost his path one day,
And turned the clay to gold.

"Silent was he! the angel came again;—
And as she passed along,
She kiss'd his lips, all lovingly — and then
He opened them in song." — *Arnold.*

PHILADELPHIA:
J. B. LIPPINCOTT & CO.
1869.

DEDICATION.

TO MY FRIEND, R. BELL, ESQ., OF PORTSMOUTH, OHIO.

[Written during his long and painful illness of 1865.]

Oh, why must the good and the pure
Suffer ills which the world cannot cure?
And the spirits best fitted to shine
On earth with a lustre divine,

Be scourged with physical pain,
And sorrow detach the rich vein
Of a life that is richer to all;
Oh, why must this trial befall?

While doing the Master's behest,
With faith that is never at rest;
With energy scorning repose,
At work for thy friends and thy foes.

With feet never faltering, though
The journey is weary we know,
To the goal far-lying and free,
And the rest that remaineth for thee.

*The world seemeth sunny and wide
To many who walk by thy side,
With hopes to which angels respond
'Mid regions of promise beyond.*

*Won back by thy precepts again
From by-paths of prayerless pain;
Many lives are worthier grown
In the light thy goodness has shown.*

*In thy mansion the orphan is blest!
There the faint and the weary find rest.
No suffering human can say,
He turned from my pleading away.*

*Or mortal can lift up his face,
In God's light of truth, with a trace
Of record 'twere best to recall —
Thy justice is meted to all!*

*Thy charity, heavenly art,
Dispensed in meekness of heart:
Thou'rt worthy to join the bright band
Who walk on the beautiful strand.*

*And, oh! when life's conflict is done,
The goal of thy merit is won,
High hearts will bow over thy tomb,
Rich blessings will follow thee home.*

*From earth-ways of penitent strife,
Through portals of death unto life,*

DEDICATION.

The meed of thy labor to gain,
A harvest of time's golden grain.

The spaces are narrowing now,
Bright fingers are fitting thy brow
To its crown! — Salvation is free.
Grace to conquer was given to thee.

Thy example lessons has taught,
Of duty — so patiently wrought
In faith and obedience to one
Who is God, the Father, and Son.

THE AUTHOR.

PREFATORY.

SONNET-ACROSTIC.

BY THE AUTHOR OF "INDA."

SHE is the tenth muse in her poesy,
   As proven by her melodies divine: —
   Linking the beauties of the other time
Like golden chain through her rich imagery.
Inweaving fact and fancy to refine —
Enforcing them to soothe and to improve —

Joined in her language of a heart of love!

Holding the mind enchanted in their thrall,
And wondering at the magic spell thus wove.
Not in the giddy throng of fashion's hall
Cares she to mingle in the worldly strife
Of vain pre-eminence: her powers come
Circling the scenes of pure domestic life —
Kindling affections in the hearts of home.

CONTENTS

	PAGE
Two	13
Wrecks	20
Hope	22
The Poet-Lovers	23
Be Brave	26
Somebody's Darling	28
Heart-Chimes in Holly-Time	30
Before the Dawn	32
Our Mission	33
Yancey Rests	36
Autumn Rain	37
The Gloria in Excelsis	39
The Cumberland	44
Home	46
To my Friend	48
Waiting	51
Divided	52

	PAGE
THE OLD AND THE NEW	53
BROWN EYES	56
IN MEMORY OF	57
TO A FRIEND	60
PROMISE	61
TO ——	62
SUNRISE	63
HOPE IN DEATH	65
MY DREAM	66
LATONA	70
BEAUTIFUL SNOW	72
ONE YEAR AGO	73
OLD AND POOR	75
SACRIFICE	77
SPRING	78
FOUR YEARS OF WAR	80
IN THE SHADOW	82
EVAN CASTLE	84
CASTE	86
ON A PORTRAIT	88
HIDDEN AWAY	90
A PRAYER	91
ARION	92
LIGHT AND DARKNESS	94
NEVERMORE	97
WILLIE LEE	99

CONTENTS.

	PAGE
IN MEMORIAM.	100
THE FEMALE PHARISEE'S SOLILOQUY	101
FIFTEENTH KENTUCKY INFANTRY	107
LITTLE PAUL	108
THE DEAD LOVE	110
DAISY-TIME	111
PAST	112
PRESENT	113
FUTURE	114
HILLS OF MAYSVILLE	115
THE MOTHER'S LAMENT	117
A SONNET	119
MAGGIE RAYMOND — SONNET	120
THE BLUE AND THE GRAY	120
TO MRS. S. V.	122
RECOMPENSE	122
THE GAY PALACE	124
THE LAST ROSE-BUD	126
SOMEWHERE	127
GENIUS	128
TO BELLE F. C.	130
TO ———	132
SONNET	133
BINGEN ON THE RHINE	134
KINDRED GRAVES	136
REDEEMED BY LOVE	138

CONTENTS

	PAGE
To E. L. S.	141
The Brown Hand	142
Justice — A Sonnet	144
To my Friend	145
Never Again	146
The Tablet	147
Summer Gone	148
John Halifax	149
"My Years Go On"	151
Rosa	153
"Shadowed Light"	154
Augustine	156
The Loved and Lost	158
Finale	159

POEMS.

TWO.

TWO lives — of soul and sense to music set;
A song of triumph and of fond regret:

Whose thoughts are in my heart this summer-day;
Whose phantoms e'er pursue the life-long way.

That which is, and that which might have been:
That which was, and ne'er can be again.

Two souls together cast before the dawn;
Two spirits mingling in the glow of morn.

Two hearts — love-joined in the first flash of light;
Two hands upraised to heav'n in human sight.

Two lives in wedlock clasped so fond and true,
Began the journey when the day was new.

Two living souls within the mortal clay;
Two spirits, young and happy, bright and gay.

Anon were joys more sweet and precious given,
And baby-feet came down the stairs of heav'n.

And earth was very glad, and we were blest;
Two lives unmindful, and two souls at rest.

Two hearts forgetful of the Giver's praise,
His wrath descended swift upon our ways.

Two lives from ours were taken back to God;
Two little forms were bedded in the sod.

Two little graves near the old home were made,
In winter white — green in the summer-shade.

Consigned our idols were to earthly mould,
The Saviour's lambs were taken to his fold.

Bright waves yet sported with the lapwing's crest;
Swift summers glided outward to the west.

Two lips said sneeringly — "My joy is o'er!"
Two eyes were bent toward the distant shore; —

Toward a fairer idol 'yond the deep,
Two waiting eyes were rarely closed in sleep.

Two lips that careless said, "Your love is vain,"
A heart that coldly thought upon my pain.

TWO.

There came no answer to my pleading prayer,
No look or tone to comfort my despair.

No answer, though from spring to spring again,
Seasons tracked the snowy-crested main.

Now stand we each on ocean-severed strands;
Between us countless waves and falling sands.

No more to meet upon the earth — no more.
The morning has gone by — the summer's o'er.

My way has been so dark and drear along
The olden paths and early flowers among.

Life holds so little worth our toil save woe,
That cuts the soul from all the faith we know.

Anon we come to do without its hopes,
And shape our course toward its peaceful slopes.

How have I supplicated strength from God,
Who smote my heart to atoms with his rod.

And he has shown to me my empty life,
Divested of its pangs and human strife;

Has sent for answer to my earnest prayer,
Those who would win a crown, a cross must bear.

Ere long the night wore slowly toward the day,
In which he took my feet from out the clay,

And planted them upon the higher ground,
Where I beheld, in calmly looking round,

The plan and purpose of my trial: saw
The greater good his love had wrought; for, ah!

His eyes had not looked coldly on my pain,
Nor was my cry of mortal anguish vain.

For he has blest me more than I can tell;
Before my eager eyes a vision fell.

I saw my destiny by his hand wrought;
The discipline was wise, thus sorely taught.

A thousand aspirations then were born,
And glided o'er the purple hills of morn.

Oh! in that darkest hour my spirit caught
Power to touch the springs of human thought.

I clearly saw two lives, the false and true,
The paltry pride whereon my pleasures grew;

The spirit-needs that hitherto had slept,
And long had slumbered, had I never wept.

The false lights go out in reason's dawn,
In whose clear beams no meager schemes are born.

No empty forms of sense can triumph o'er
The pure bright shapes we worship evermore;

Or gain the promise which the future brings,
To all who labor for the higher things; —

To which his love would wed us, if we knew
How to receive them, and were faithful too.

His forms of truth stand ever clear and bright;
All that is false will crumble in the sight

Of the fairer vision his mercy shows —
That of a spirit purged by human throes.

My hands, O Lord, are ready for thy task;
To serve thee now, I humbly only ask.

Thine own for me hast swept a magic string,
And taught my wayward lips the way to sing;

Hast opened in my heart a crystal fount,
And taught the sprite of poesy to mount,

On airy pinions from life's deserts drear,
To where the sunshine is so bright and clear;

Hast filled my desolation with the things
Ne'er purchased by the gold or blood of kings;

Set sweet eternal music in my soul,
Whose sounding echoes ever round me roll.

The gift vouchsafed to me of human speech!
Shall I employ it so my words will reach —

Through the to-come — adown time's mazy line,
Revealing unto some a hidden shrine;

Discovering to blinded heart and eyes —
A lighthouse in the mind, that will uprise,

And shine upon the ruins of life's plain,
To guide the wanderer back to thee again.

Oh! if one pilgrim shall find quiet rest,
Along the beaten way my feet have prest;

If one draught from this fountain pure and clear
Has quenched a thirstful longing vain and drear;

That my poor hand has lifted to the lips,
So pallid in their blighted hope's eclipse;

If I have shown to one the hidden gleam,
Lost in the mazes of some fond, vain dream;

If I, one chord have swept, of deep, pure joy,
Of friendship constant, love without alloy,

The mighty deathless love, whose firm strong arm
Can lull a restless spirit with its charm,

Can shelter all who come within its reach: —
Be this my recompense — the gift of speech.

Thrice blest my work, in making others blest,
In doing which my soul has found sweet rest.

My mission has not been in vain!—anon,
Perchance, some spirit, loved in years bygone,

Will read what I have written—and at last,
With heart true throbbing to the buried past,

Say then—"I never knew her, even when
I claimed her. Oh! were she mine again,

I would hold her more worthy of the love,
Which lonely trial-years do not disprove,

Or rifle of its truth: that which to gain,
Has shown to me my sacrifice was vain."

'Twas very hard without his love to live;
'Tis easy now to tell him, I forgive.

These words the years have taught me how to speak;
They have not bowed me down, or paled my cheek,

Or quenched the latent fire within mine eyes,
Upraised in faith unto God's morning skies.

I see new glory in the forms they wear,
Of patient duty, and the fruits they bear.

I, too, shall cross an ocean dark and wide,
Bright spirits beckon from the farther side;

E'er fond and true, they wait me where I go,
The journey ended, and my task below,

And all that might have been — perhaps may be —
My faith has crossed before life's twilight sea.

I'll to these broken hopes, yon portal crost,
Exclaim, "Poor dreams, not worth the tears you cost."

The tribute of each thought I bear to thee,
Who broke the bonds and set my spirit free.

My sweetest songs are those which hymn thy praise,
Thou God, our great Redeemer, all my days.

The truest life was that which humbly grew,
Flowers of toil and trust the life-way through,

Whose privilege and seed-time are to-day,
Whose harvest-season is — eternity.

WRECKS.

ANY shattered wrecks strew God's creation!
    Dun deserts creep where flowers were wont
       to grow;
And lie along the beaten shores of nations —
  A never-ending record of unworded woe,
    While time's great ages course their varying flow.

WRECKS.

Down where the coral glories flash and quiver,
   'Mid chill expanses of the murmuring deep;
And where bright broken sunbeams pale and shiver
   On the cold tract, where gathered twilights weep,
   A million wrecks lie wrapt in dreamless sleep.

And there are human wrecks deep in our feeling!
   We only 'mid desolation heard their sigh,
And kissed the lips white, with their last appealing,
   Ere fate had stilled at length the wailing cry,
   Touchingly plaintive as a "prayer gone by."

In our hearts where those poor wrecks are sleeping,
   Comes no moon or star-beam to the waveless main;
No morning with its trailing glories keeping
   Sweet watch above our spirit's silent pain,
   And sorrow for the trust we ne'er can know again.

And yet, O Father! thy great heart is bowing
   Now with the weight of every human woe.
Though fire, and wreck, and pain, and wrong allowing,
   Through these brief days of mortal time, we know
   Thou art the Lord! Thine ages come and go.

Worthless idols to which our souls are clinging
   Now flash bright radiance, then go out apace.
Ah! list above the wrecks; hear voices singing,
   "This is not all of life—the world-bound race,
   Whose mazy paths through sin and fire we trace.

"Anon will all the flameful wrath abating,
   Reveal the glory of a happier day;

From deserts dun with care and gloomy waiting,
    We will return some morning, nevermore to stray
From the quiet sunshine of a better way.

"We lose not all in parting from earth's treasure,
    With tearful agony, and groan, and cry;
There is a sweet love-life of boundless measure,
    An inner temple radiant, looming high;
'A house not made with hands' beyond the sky.

"There is a world with vales of light outshining
    The brightest Edens which we seek in this;
Where hearts nor lives hold wrecks nor useless pining,
    Nor lips long vaguely for a vanished kiss,
    Nor storms, nor fire sweep o'er that land of bliss."

HOPE.

SWEET hope! most precious boon to mortals given,
    Thou golden link between the earth and heaven;
Thou beacon in the port of ocean wide,
Thou lighthouse gleaming on the farther side;
Thou landmark on the rugged way below,
Thou sister twin of all the joy we know.

Thou spring of youth to mortals gray and old,
Thou summer to our winters bleak and cold;

Thou meteor, meet to light the twilight gray,
Thou radiant star upon a darksome way;
Thou sun of all the universal light!
Thou morning breaking on the shores of night;
Thou promise in affliction — joy in health,
Our present treasure, and our future wealth.
Thou pure white bud of paradisal bloom,
Thou rainbow-span above our mortal tomb;
Heart, soul, and mind do unto thee respond,
Thou glory of the world, and heaven beyond!

THE POET LOVERS.

"One life, one love, one death, one immortality." — SHELLEY.

DREAMS, "languor-steeped in gold,".
   And "tranced in summer-calm,"
     Gleam, aureola-like, and odor-filled,
Upon a wide, wild waste of memory.
Like palms of air on sand, robins hold
Their *matinee* within the tufted wold —
Fragrant with perfumes and wild-lotus blooms —
As when the poet first his story told,
With truth that pierced of truth the living soul.

They lived an age of glory in their pride!
They loved each other more than worlds beside —
More than the pageantry that waits on fame;
More than the glitter of a splendid name;

More than the luminance of brain-bought gold;
More than o'er words of inspiration told.
Yet love to them was shadowed as the day,
Mist-touched, and prematurely old,
And gray amid life's gathering glooms,
With the fell pallor of earth's poet-tombs.

    The harvest-moon was new;
    A sickle hanging high,
A horn of amber blazing on the sky,
While "heaven flowed in through many dreams:"
    The twilight softer grew —
    One star flashed out anigh;
Coquettish smiles on night, as if to woo,
With all the timid splendor of her beams,
Those loyal hearts aloft while pulsing true,
They clasped eternity in one last hour —
All the bliss and madness of love's power
O'er time. The moments full-blazoned grew —
As glory-hallowed they flitted by.

            A barren reach of world
Around, *and death between!* From moon to moon
Earth's flame-tipped banners wave unfurled
Like thoughts with fire agleam.
Too soon fulfilled the heaven-born dream,
When fate her burning falchion hurled
Adown the grooves of doom. Too soon
    A godly heart was stilled!
    Mists flock th' empurpled hills,
    And bright-winged oriole trills

His summer chant unheard. The moon,
As then, with splendor lights the sleeping world!
Again for him the golden star shall beam
In heaven's dimless noon.

   For her? Death over all
Cast the fell shadow of his darksome pall.
 Slowly the cycle paled —
 The golden star was veiled!
No more at evening did her heart rejoice,
No more in song was heard her clarion voice.
Grim silence shut the music in;
A wall of blackness hid the silver fall
Of light. *Her life's one melody —*
The airy palm — the swallows flitting by —
Henceforth, were as they had not been

Froze was the vein of inspiration in her soul,
Though she toiled bravely for the nearing goal.
Weary, alas! and yet not where to rest.
Cold was the pillow once her head had pressed.
Through the leal heart her priceless love had blessed,
Rank grasses grew above the poet's breast.

While waiting for the end, her calm look said, —
"A thousand lives are nothing — *he is dead!*"
Faith wrote on her pale brow these words, — "I know
My love — God gives him back to me — I go."
Then, she too slept! and blent in one glad flow
Their loves and songs. The broken lyres below.

BE BRAVE.

AH! coward soul, why fear betray?
  With heart to love and lip to pray,
  Thou shouldst not shrink or turn away —
    God holds the issue fast.
Still, then, thy wild, rebellious cry;
With unblanched face and tearless eye
Resolve, whatever comes, to try
    And win the crown at last.

Oh! craven spirit, dost thou esteem
Far brighter than a heavenly gleam,
One glance of eyes whose splendors beam
    With a transcendent love?
And is the clasp of one dear hand
More to thy heart than the bright band
Who at the gates of glory stand
    To welcome thee above?

More than white robe or shining crown,
Or tuneful chorus pealing down
The ages, with their mellow brown
    Of harvest waving free;
Than walking through the golden street,
Where all the saints and angels meet!
Is this companionship more sweet
    Than such could ever be?

To feel that heaven is *here, and now,*
And come to give it up, and bow
In dust a pallid, crownless brow.
    "Yet, Father, it shall be!
Though heart should break, and weary cry
Should rend my soul, yet will I try
To drink — the cup may not pass by : —
    Be merciful to me."

What though temptation gird about,
My trustful life with clinging doubt,
And the alluring bliss without
    The sacrificial pale :
And sweet lips wooing bid me come;
And fond heart tells of other home;
And love which underneath the dome
    Of heaven shall never fail.

The heights of truth I must attain,
And stand above the clinging stain
Of time. E'en though the dream was vain —
    'T was pure and very sweet.
The love was holy in thy sight,
A spirit of celestial might,
A presence radiantly bright —
    For heaven truly meet.

Yet God's was greater! and how vain
Is human worship while the stain
Of earthiness, decay, and pain,
    Rests on the life we hold;

And all its rare bright shapes and fair,
Must wither in the charnel air,
On low still dreamless pillows where
   They slumber 'neath the mould.

Where love and hate, with sigh and tear,
And craven-hearted coward fear,
Are hidden with the darkness drear,
   Away from human sight.
E'en though a silent feast is spread,
In memory of the loved and dead,
The narrow house and coffin-bed:
   Behold! the promise bright—

Breaks over all life's brooding years;
The Christian's trials, and his tears:
The Christian's hopes, the Christian's fears.
   The pitying Saviour-friend,
Who lit with stars the twilight gray,
Who took from death the sting away,
Will give us heart and lip to pray,
   "God sanctify the end."

"SOMEBODY'S DARLING."

OVER the mountain, and over the river,
   Where spaces are merged in morning's bright
      blue;
Down where the cuckoo birds beckon and quiver;
Somebody's darling is waiting for you.

"SOMEBODY'S DARLING."

Somebody's pet in the noon and the night,
Raises a face all glowing and bright;
Somebody's hands are outstretched to greet.
Hear you the patter of somebody's feet?
Over the garden-way, down by the tombs,
Where the tall stones glisten white through the
    glooms!
Somebody's loved one goes to the gate;
Somebody whispers *your name* while we wait.
Somebody says at the close of each day,—
"Oh! could he know how for his coming we pray."

All through the long summer you've linger'd afar!
Now at the rising of yonder bright star,
Somebody despairs—and the moon seems to say,
As she bends her fair brow to the star, "let us pray."
All trembling the star gives for answer—"I'll sing,
That the light of our morrow the absent may bring."

Over the mountain, and over the river,
Up to the throne of the gracious All-giver!
On the bright wings of a spirit most true,
Borne through the arcades of heaven for you.
That song and petition the world may not hear,
Is caught by the grace of the father's quick ear,
And soon will be answered. Faith says, await
Still the unwinding this coil of our fate.
In the here, or hereafter, ever be true,
Somebody's darling lives only for you.
Somebody's loved one will clasp, as before,
Your hand in the now, or the great evermore.

"It shall be in the now," — a quick voice replies;
Somebody's darling is sweetly surprised;
Somebody's lips to be pressed are full fain;
Somebody's guest will not leave us again.
For heart, soul, and brain are too weary to roam,
If they only find rest in somebody's home,
Peace in the shelter of somebody's love,
And the path leading up to the mansion above.

HEART-CHIMES IN HOLLY-TIME.

WE are waiting, brother, patiently awaiting!
To feel thy fond, fond, kiss upon our cheek;—
And words of welcome breathe, we fain would speak
To thee who hast grim tides of battle —
Breasted bravely since our last-time greeting.
   We are waiting, patiently awaiting.

We are waiting, brother, hopefully awaiting!
Within our dear old home the childhood-light —
Is burning cheerily for thee to-night.
Seasons weary since our New-Year parting,
Changes many since our last fond greeting.
   We are waiting, hopefully awaiting.

We are waiting, brother, anxiously awaiting!
Ever through the long, long night we're pining.
Thou com'st not while sweet stars are shining,

HEART-CHIMES IN HOLLY-TIME.

Nor yet at morning in the glory-light,
And when the sunshine and the day are waning,
   We are waiting, anxiously awaiting.

We are waiting, brother, tearfully awaiting!
White as snow our mother's cheek is paling,
While listening to the chill winds wailing —
Blighting holly-wreaths, heart-lights burn faintly;
Chill night-dews fall, sweet hope is dying.
   We are waiting, tearfully awaiting.

We are waiting, brother, hopelessly awaiting!
Only a letter came with words of yearning;
"Be patient, mother dear, I am not coming;
No leave of absence yet — no home returning —
For me no Christmas chimes, no hearth-light burning.
   Ever waiting, hopelessly awaiting."

Hark! hear the watch-dog bark! we are not waiting.
We hear a manly voice so soft and tender,
We raise our own to meet thy dark eyes' splendor;
Soul-music swells — merry chimes are pealing;
Lights are brighter, and the hearth-stone glowing.
   Thank God! we are not waiting, vainly waiting.

BEFORE THE DAWN.

DEAR mother, the shadows are long,
   On the plains of the slumberous world;
   The brooks lie asleep in the arms of the night,
The broad-breasted river rests peaceful and white,
On a cradle of infinite calm,—and the wind,
   Like the nightingale, sings a wild song.

   Sweet mother, love's tribute I bring;
Though a silence broods dumb in my heart.
Whose brooks once were gleesome, whose oceans aheave,
Whose tides of emotion, I surely believe,
Are now sweeping on to the shore, where we grieve
   Never more while the orioles sing.

   For souls in the shadow of night
Cannot stay from their home in the sky,
Where a twilight e'er closes our sunniest day;
And where 'mid the blight and the gloom of the way,
We build our bright fanes of the veriest clay,
   And cover their shrines from our sight.

   Dear mother, the night may reach on!
For the life-time is only begun:
Yet the infinite love that is ours in the dark—
Of our way through the world is the heavenly arc
That will bear o'er the waters our wandering bark
   As it nears the white shores of the dawn.

Till down through the ages will stream,
The glories we dream of afar:
Where the mountains of promise reach higher and
    higher,
'Yond the "pillar of cloud and the pillar of fire;"
And the opaline gleam of a heavenly spire
    Rises clear in eternity's beam.

OUR MISSION.

A METRICAL ESSAY.

ALL who were born upon the earth,
    Time's servitors — heirs of immortal birth,
    Since first the heritors of Eden prest
Its scented turf, have here a mission blest
    By the Creator's sanction.

    This day of earth is only lent,
Till we have wrought his purpose; — being sent
To live — perform, to suffer and repent,
And come to him at last with our account
Well balanced! Strike off mortal fetters — mount
    Time's heights to hear the sweet "Well done."

    Hence, patient and faithful ever,
Thou humble worker at some home fireside;
Thy lowly lot and destiny abide.
There thou may'st learn a secret better worth —

Than gold of kings—the marvel of thy birth.
God holds of life thy simple plan.

Pale wanderer in distant climes,
Why seekest thou to murder years he gave?
Hopeless and aimless thy journey to the grave.
And are his gifts to thee so little worth,
That thou shouldst find no pleasure on the earth,
No work in all the busy land?

All human things are strangely changed,
Since the first fires were kindled great and high
Upon the sunset-shrines of Eden. Why
Are there few sages in the nowadays,
To concentrate of wisdom her pure rays
For those who only sit and wait?

Why must a man win all the world,—
Serve fame, ambition, fortune, caprice, all,
Before he cares to speak for God, or call
Upon his Master's name with sanctity,—
Till he, poor worm, shall come at last to see,
His wasted opportunity?

Oh! patient teacher, kind and true,
For this hast thou set humble workers here,
Who serve thee earnestly without the fear
Of losing what such paltry souls may win,—
The gilded homage of this age of sin.
Strive they for higher, better things?

In the still vineyards of the Lord,
Many are set to work, and some to teach
The humble few whom wisdom may not reach.
Oh! least of all his people, be ye wise!
From simplest deeds may influences rise,
    That dwell in hearts for evermore.

And thus it strangely came to pass,
That simple lips were taught to utter truths
That are enduring;—messages of ruth
Have flowed through channels unforetold
By priest or prophet in the days of old.
    Hail! women of the latter day—

Whose lips teach us to preach and pray;
Whose feeble hand may leave upon the years,
Beside the record of her burning tears,
Words of inspiration — heaven-caught,
Which show us earth and Christ as suffering wrought
    For her the revelation.

When having won a patient ear,
Will tell the simple story of the cross:
The greater suffering—the greater loss
Which that dear Saviour bore, whose love to save
Poor wanderers from a cruel death and grave—
    Of sin, his precious life he gave.

    Oh! more than human love was this.
Oh! touching story which a child may feel.
Who may not tell it, who may not reveal

The mystery some potent hand has stirred?
Impelled to utterance the facts averred
   That teach us *here are life and love.*

The world is wide, God far away,
Unless we have some mission in our lives
Of good to others every day, which strives
To aid the weak and erring, help them o'er
Time's wide, rough ocean, to the shining shore
   Whose borders are the yet to be.

YANCEY RESTS.

ON a hillock rising fair,
   Wrapt about with starlit dreams,
   Gloaming shadows hover there,
And the darkness darker seems.

Back unto the olden life,
   Peaceful tides are coursing slow;
Free from terror, dash, and strife,
   O'er the proud head lying low.
Softly 'neath the amber sun,
   Spice-winds blow and palm-trees wave:
Though his rest was nobly won,
   Ceaseless twilight shrouds his grave.

Oh! the silence long and deep,
   Stretching to eternal morn.

Never broken be that sleep
On his country's heart forlorn.
Great souls bowing felt the stroke,
When his heart in sorrow broke.

AUTUMN RAIN.

OH! patter, patter; list the ceaseless rain,
  Upon the roof, a melancholy strain;
  A constant tattoo, never out of time:
The soft sedate contralto of my rhyme,
Whose tidal music, ever coursing on
Beneath the cold dark arch of years bygone,
Breaks dreamily upon my work, and lo!
Strange fancies woo me as they come and go.

Though bowing 'neath the weight of sordid things,
I wander through the blight of many springs
To one so very fair, so long gone by,
Where hope shone sweetly in the morning sky;
And there was other music in the day
Than falling rain upon life's lightsome way.
No breath had chill'd, as now, the early flow'rs,
No burning tears fell through the autumn hours.

Ah! then I loved to hear the cold drops fall,
Like human tears upon the summer's pall,

And see the sere leaves flutter on the air,
Like birds unmated, drifting anywhere.
But oh! when dearest hopes like these take flight,
And soar beyond the range of human sight:
When other bitter drops like flowers fall,
And mist of mortal tears is over all,
There is such pathos in the sad refrain,
Such mellow music in the autumn rain.

Love of my soul, inanimate and still!
Myriad voices once proclaimed at will
The hopes and dreams that were so vainly vain.
The heart, now lorn and lonely in its pain,
Was glad; with strong deep pulses bounding free,
And joyous with exultant constancy.
O silent throbs! O passion wild and vain!
Thy flowers fall beneath the autumn rain.
O solemn day, so full of longing now!
O record of thy pain upon my brow!
O broken dreams! thy graves are everywhere.
Seas hold thy forms of old; and boundless air
Is filled with shapes so exquisitely fair.
Ne'er hidden in a tomb where I might bow,
And kiss the pure white chaplet faded now.
They glided 'neath the same cold arch at last,
Along the silent way my dead ones passed;
Yet gave no promises to soothe my pain,
That I might ever dream those dreams again.

I shudder for my dead, outlying where
No heart of mine can shelter them fore'er.

I know the Father guards them, though I weep;
For, oh! "he giveth his beloved sleep."
And yet I long to clasp them once again,
Those patient sleepers 'neath the autumn rain.

Now over all the mist and mortal blight,
Though trust is shining sweetly on the height
Of faith, the path is lone and drear,
Marked by many an agonizing tear.
And yet I know it leads to peace again,—
Though winter should succeed the autumn rain.
Vistas of summer lie beyond! and soon
Will ope the portals of some fairy June,
That is eternal; where, through Jesus' grace,
We'll find in his great love a genial place;
Unmarked by loss, as in this age of pain,
Or clinging cross, or scourging autumn rain.

THE GLORIA IN EXCELSIS.

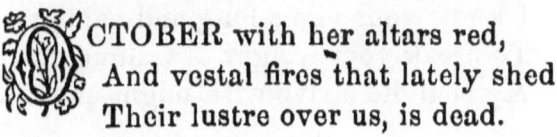

OCTOBER with her altars red,
And vestal fires that lately shed
Their lustre over us, is dead.

The autumn fields lie crisp and bare;
On ways of earth are gloom and care,
And flitting shadows everywhere.

Like bronze appears the golden maize,
And fallen leaves have hid the ways
To woodland shrines of prayer and praise.

I list in vain one birdling's trill,
Or silver voice of sunny rill;
The upland brook is locked and still.

Alas! that earth should fail to keep
The least of all her glories: — weep!
Ours leave us for a longer sleep.

Upon the smallest thing I read,
Just what the inner prompting said,
A resurrection from the dead.

Thus nature doth rehearse the plan
Of free salvation, life to man:
Her seasons must be born again.

O world, with all your clinging mould,
And ceaseless strife for paltry gold,
How much of loss and pain you hold!

I know your vigils long and vain;
To break your weight of galling chain
My soul did strive with might and main.

The images my heart did make,
Some cruel hand of fate did shake,
Or stern iconoclast did break.

I wore the fetters yet a while,
Then laid the broken shapes of guile
Down at my Saviour's feet. A smile

Gave he in answer to each tear,
Until, upon my doubt and fear,
A star of faith rose bright and clear,

Upon the mazes of the way:
I quenched my thirsting in the spray
Of fountain pure as rising day.

A voice rose clear above the din: —
"There is a life which you may win,
Whose hidden wealth lies all within."

I opened wide the doors of mind,
To seek the treasure I designed.
I asked of God, and he was kind.

He saw my needs, and gave me all
The boundless riches of a soul
His hands had made for my control.

Now, while I consecrate my gift,
Some mystic power has seemed to sift
From life the useless passing drift,

And left the current bright and free
Of thought. I can no longer be
The slave of time and misery.

I seem to feel a presence near
Just up above me in the clear
Bright shimmer of the heavenly air.

A radiant something at my side:
A hand touch mine, as if to guide
Aright my pen, some angel tried.

Here, in my lone retreat, I seem
To catch the distant glory-gleam
Of many a paradisal dream.

I long to speak with other tongue,
And then to hear God's praises rung
The multitudes of earth among.

I think I list with other ear
The music of that higher sphere,
That home so far, and yet so near;

And oft behold, with other eyes,
The glimmer of the inner skies,
Through outer domes of paradise.

The crystal water gleaming wide,
The radiant shore beyond the tide,
And footprints of the glorified.

Below me lie the plains of earth,
With gliding pageant scarcely worth
The faintest hope of higher birth.

THE GLORIA IN EXCELSIS.

I had a dream: it was so strange,
A love that never cared to range
Burned clearer in the fires of change.

'Twas not for me. Now I repent
That I repined. It was not sent:
The passing vision came and went.

Oh! friends so true, through gliding years,
Whose hearts have borne my rain of tears,
Whose radiant faces light my fears!

These are my helpers! — my delight! —
My compensation meet and right,
O Father, in thy blessed sight.

These are the works my clearer sight
Has shown to me. A path of light
Streams out upon the shores of night.

No ripple seems to stir the air,
So filled with melody, as 't were
A role of triumph rich and rare.

I lay aside my earth-worn guise, —
My soul is full of glad surprise;
My thoughts in prayerful anthems rise.

And now a hope is swift to start,
Soft, like an echo, in my heart,
That I may win a nobler part,

And place amid God's working throng,
Borne to those shining gates along,
By the sweet magic of a song

Whose cadence rings through all my days.
The burden-chant of all my lays —
Shall be this song of love and praise.

THE CUMBERLAND.

THE sun sank calmly on thy breast;
  Mist gathered in the glowing west,
  Round Edgefield's spires. The night was still.
The moon came out o'er College Hill:
With floods of golden arrows bright
Wooed thy deeps to waves of light —

Shone clearly on the sentry's beat,
Mid camp-fires blazing in the street;
And gilding Negley's summit star,
And banner proudly floating there —
A talisman to all who prize,
And view our flag with moistened eyes —

When out upon the picket-line,
So stilly in the cold moonshine,
They listened for the faintest sound;
Then rushing deathward with a bound,
When swift convulsion, boding harm,
Should change this starlit calm to storm.

Above yon tented walls, at night,
The Capitol stands ghastly white.
In many a far, far home is woe,
Momentoed in the vale below,
Where break thy waves in graceful spray
To music in the closing day.

Dream on, brave heroes, silently!
Glide on, bright river, to the sea!
The pride of north and southern lands,
The joy of broken household bands;
True hearts, that bled at every pore,
Lie buried on thy starlit shore.

Peace was abroad! in dreams that night,
I saw cold hearth-stones gleaming bright;
Loved ones at home amid the throng
Who felt their absence, oh! how long;
And saw the dead just passing o'er
Thy tides unto God's golden shore;—

Saw brothers linking heart and hand
In union on that lovelit strand;
No war-drawn front nor vigils there,
No breaking hearts for them to share;
No blood-bought peace or red-brow'd Mars
To pluck from thee thy mirror'd stars.

HOME.

OVER a track where the dead leaves lie,
  The home-bound train doth fleetly fly;
  The plains are ruddy, and reeds of gold,
Like sun-bars, lattice heather and wold.
Where purple altheas glance and quiver,
The sinuous trail of many a river,
Is bridged by the feet that trample down
Wayside flowers in country or town.

Loud tones of the engine deft and shrill,
Wake echoes grand from valley and hill;
Whirling along through woodland and field,
With crash of iron and clank of steel.
Livid bolts of fire that rise and fall,
Through the pallid glare that is over all.
The pause — the shadow of night amain
The starless mist and the driving rain, —

And the drifting cloudlets vapor-hung:
O'er still dark woods was the echo rung,
"*Of home sweet home,*" while the train swept on,
Leaving the grace of a vision gone —
Like vanished day from the mountain side,
Where a fordless river, deep and wide,
Crept slowly on to the ocean-tide.

Silence o'er time in the growing space,
Fell like a shroud on a loved dead face.
I dreamed in the clasp of memory,
With a phantom bright for company:
A beauteous shape that glided away,
And left me alone in the night to pray
For the rising moon, or the dawn of day.

Now over the spaces far out on the night,
Flash glittering moonbeams silvery white;
Trembling—drifting, while golden stars quiver
Down in the heart of the luminous river,
Singing again on its way—forever.

   'Time spares age nor youth!
     Clasped hands—plighted hearts
       Earth may dissever:
    Change curses the world!
    God's grace is love's truth!
    God's love life imparts,
     "His mercy" is ruth—
       And "endureth forever."'

Over the deserts of woodland and wold;
Glowing in summer, in winter bleak cold;
Over the reaches of land and of wave,
Linking existence from cradle to grave!
God's is the power all potent to save—
Worlds from the wreck of their votaries blind,
Hearts from their breaking, souls truly shrined

In caskets of truth from sorrow and pain;
By strength of their love, reunited again.

Oh, in the light of our beautiful star,
And moon gleaming white on summit and spar,
Over the path *bright with truth,* darling, come:
For us 'tis the better, the only way home.
There's waiting for hearts, and work day by day,
For God and the world! yet a luminous ray
Of hope gilds desert and wave. Be our rest —
Our home on starlighted shores of the blest.
All life's but a day, and at evening we'll glide
To the angelic haven of love — side by side.

TO MY FRIEND,

MRS. EDMUND J. DAUMONT, OF LOUISVILLE, KENTUCKY.

WHEN over all this wide and weary world,
  Were cast grave shadows of a buried trust;
  And sable banners of despair unfurled,
Where love's fair shapes were stricken into dust,
Thy spirit linked with mine, sat by the grave
  Where my sad heart lay silent, past rebound:
'Twas thy sweet lips that said, "Dear friend, be brave,
  Our Father's love will heal the bleeding wound.

"From out the gloaming darkness light will spring!
  The chaos into beauteous order grow;

TO MY FRIEND.

The tiny bird of peace, with radiant wing,
   Will circle all those hours of rayless woe,
In which the lovelight of thy blighted life
   Faded, while tears, bitter and swift, fell down.
Through years of waiting, and of spirit-strife,
   Thy portion is the cross, be thine the crown."

That crown of promise sitting by thy side,
   To win it, thou hast shown to me the way;
But oh! the spaces seem so far and wide,
   And night around me lowers cold and gray,
Though thy sweet love has fail'd, or falter'd ne'er,
   But brightened all my darkness like a star.
No fate dividing us, save death I fear;
   No blight to come can e'er that glory mar.

Now let the great world spin its endless course,
   From winter unto winter back again;
Let other storm-winds blow with cruel force,
   And drench us with their scourging chill and rain.
Our love shall stand all tests of coming time,
   E'er "firm and steadfast"—watchwords of the strong;
Linked, thy sweet songs unto my untaught rhyme,
   Forming bright chains of truth enduring long.

Truth that has been fore'er, my shield and joy;
   Making thee all-glorious as thou art:
It beams from out the clear eyes of thy boy,
   And lightens many a sad and weary heart.

Thy brow is radiant with its holy trace,
   Its spirit-fingers touch thy soft, brown hair;
If ever worth sat on a human face,
   Then does thine own, sweet friend, its impress wear.

And oh! perchance, when I shall pass away,
   And earth shall hold no longer any trace
Of what has been, then let thy dear feet stray
   To the still mound uprisen o'er my face.
Remembering all the past,— *our past*,— the days
   When thy sweet love was half the world to me.
And know my heart is blessing thee always,
   My spirit lingering ever near to thee.

Teach darling Eddie to remember too,
   How his sweet prattle bound him to my heart;
And thy bright home, whose quiet pleasures grew
   To be of my sad life so dear a part.
I would not linger on in dreary pain,
   A waiting pilgrim, when thy work is done:
My life of sacrifice would seem so vain,
   My journey lonely toward the setting sun.

Sweet friend, the strife is past! 't is over now,
   The better way I've found 'mid grief and tears.
Life's noon lies radiant on the mountain's brow,
   To which I climbed those lonely, loveless years
Of toil and loss and pain. I see beyond
   The summit, stars of Zion gleaming where
They said I should behold them. Farther on
   "A rest remaineth,"— we will seek it there.

WAITING.

WAITING where life found us
    Through its weary day,
    With its seas around us
Moaning drearily.
Waiting in the starshine
    Of a cruel dark.
Oh! the constant soul-pine
    For the spirit-arc.

Hearts so sadly waiting
    On this lower strand
For some love to guide them
    To the better land.
Seeking — never finding;
    Waiting all the way
For the swift unwinding
    Of life's mystery.

Through the season's waiting,
    Joys we never know:
Desire never sating
    In time's sullen flow.
While the sands are falling
    On the passing shore,
See the dawn-light breaking
    In the evermore.

DIVIDED.

THERE is a glamour in the autumn air;
A mist of purple sunshine hanging fair;
And golden on the steeples, lifting high,
Their glittering turrets in the hazy sky;
A shadow on the earth — a phantom dread,
That he — the life of my love's life — *is dead.*

Cold hands press mine in slumber; and a form
Most spectral chills my blood so rich and warm,
With face as white as polar snows; the lips
Are sweetly smiling as in time's eclipse
Eternity had shown him strangely blent,
Love's finite mystery with the infinite.

O God, I thought not it was "unto death,"
That last fond parting when his heated breath
Came gushing faint and swift; the restless eye,
Where love's sweet madness burned too fatally,
Looked yet with calm and patient truth in mine,
With human tenderness almost divine.

For him to die, and I not near, to press
His pallid cheek as in one last caress,
I bid the wrathful fever cease to burn,
While brain and soul and being fondly yearn
To lay his head upon my breaking heart,
And tell him how I loved him, ere we part.

To feel upon my brow his mystic touch,
To realize the love that suffered much.
To hear once more, 'neath God's eternal sun,
The words of trust that blent our lives in one:
To clasp him closely, that the death-cold tide
Might bear us "o'er the river"—side by side.

To sleep together in some quiet spot,
Where odors of the wild forget-me-not
Will stir our grave-grass in the autumn sere,
And fill the air with heaven's fragrance there.
To know no waking from that painless rest,
Than years of life apart, 'twould be more blest.

. . . .

His "*life in death*," means, *death in life for me!*
There's mockery in each happy scene I see.
No tale of home on any face I meet,
In all the concourse through the noontide street.
That soul has soared away, that glory's orbed,
The world's great heart is still: through him it throbb'd.

THE OLD AND THE NEW.

ANOTHER year has crossed the rolling river,
    On the suspended bridge of many sighs,
    And upward to thy throne, oh! great All-giver,
Trembling prayers from living millions rise:

For that rude chains were broken, and the fetters
    Of many sordid things are cleft in twain ;
And weights from off sore hearts, and glowing letters
    Deep wrought in blood, show us the clinging stain
Of sacrifice upon the snowy pillow,
    Where the worn dotard laid his dying head,
Stricken so still and wan. The unreturning billow
    Has borne him over — the old year is dead.

He sleepeth now beneath time's grave-strewn valley,
    Where others rest, the warfare safely o'er;
The strife is ended, he no more shall rally,
    To stem life's battle-current as of yore.
Yet, oh! what spirits brave are wailing sadly;
    What loving human hearts are breaking slow;
What silent, silent tones are striving madly
    Above the spoiler-king now lying low,
For words to tell the all that he has taken,
    Of treasures which they fondly thought to keep;.
Of hopes decaying swift — spirits forsaken
    Who envy the old year his dreamless sleep.

What garlands withered we have wildly woven ;
    What blossoms faded in the spring-time gone ;
What temples fallen, and what pure shapes cloven
    With solemn blight, and wastes the snows adorn.
What dreams were broken in the sad awaking
    From fitful spirit-slumbers, void of rest ;
What glories paling slow and altars quaking
    'Neath desecrated off'rings — sin-caressed.
Oh! in the summer gone, how many reapers
    Have garnered tares in lieu of golden grain ;

What opportunities are lost, and idle sleepers
   Unhearing ever the great life-refrain!

Whose tones are not all grief-tones in the music;
   Some notes thrill to the touch of fingers bright,
And blessings swift descend with light, infusing
   A radiance serene as stars of night.
We can forget anon the broken sceptres
   We hoped to wield in kingdoms of the heart;
And how the warning rule of fate's preceptors,
   Who thus the master's lessons do impart,
Made us forego some phantom wildly chasing,
   Yet filled the void with lesser, purer things;
And while the record of our wrong erasing,
   The fruit of sacrifice unfailing brings.

We steep our souls in founts of love unceasing!
   Then lips which care had rendered thin and wan
Proclaim the life anew — with joy increasing
   Each noble impulse glowing as the morn.
With mien of courtly grace the day advances!
   O glorious face of a new year to see;
Whose dimless lustre the pure mind entrances,
   With spirit-glimpses of the life to be!
O may the fetters fall, and souls, renewing
   Their covenant of faith, be strong and true
To wage a patient warfare, humbly doing
   The noble work the Master set to do.

Old year, upon thy shrine we lay our tribute
   Of unseen tears for what with thee has gone.

Brave hearts may tremble, yet they ne'er exhibit
   One trace of all the struggle whence was born
The quiet strength of purpose, underlying
   The smallest wish of ours to do and dare
For God and for the world, by meekly trying
   To be more steadfast in our work and prayer.
Anear thy tomb we plant the simple flowers,
   Which bloom — and latest wither on the way.
Perchance their fragrance in the heav'nly bowers
   May sweeten there a never-ending day.

BROWN EYES.

INSCRIBED TO MISS JULIA CHAMBERLIN, OF LOUISVILLE, KY., WHOSE EXQUISITE PERSONAL LOVELINESS IS ONLY EQUALLED BY HER GRACE AND BEAUTY OF MIND AND CHARACTER.

IF yon worlds in the spaces we see
   Should vouchsafe their treasures to me,
   That I might embellish the shrine
Of thy beauty with tribute divine,—
Very paltry the off'ring would seem,
Compared to the splendors which beam,
And the boundless glories that rise
From the depths of thy luminous eyes.

"*Bronze-brown*" — with soft lashes of jet
In the dew of sweet radiance wet;

Scarce veiling those temples of light,
Where thy soul holds a carnival bright
Of the shapes that are rarest. Brown eyes,
Now melting with dazzling surprise,
Now flashing with mirth ; and anon
Breaking forth like the light of a morn
Half hidden in shadow. Bright eyes,
Where a slumberous mystery lies.
Sweet eyes, may thy light ever beam
Like the soul of some exquisite dream,
Bright'ning glooms that lie on the way,
Till we soar to the pure "upper day."

There's a light in my heart like the sheen
That lies brooding so spell-like, serene,
On the gems of their lustre divine.
Brown eyes, the sweet magic is thine.

IN MEMORY OF

A BRAVE SOLDIER, WHO, AFAR IN THE LAND OF THE STRANGER, LAY
DOWN TO SLEEP, TO AWAIT THE REVEILLE OF THE ETERNAL MORNING.

AUTUMN-woods are growing russet
 In the gorgeous purple sunset
  Of the waning day.
Sad we're thinking how the sunshine,
From thy far-off home, at noon-time
  Went with thee away.

Summer, then, was in the heather,
Flowers fair, and sunny weather;
      Hearts with loving light,
Saddened by the farewell spoken,
Gladdened by no coming token —
      Broken ere the night.

Oh! to think that thou wert lying,
As the autumn-leaves were dying,
      On the forest-mould,
Homeless, tentless in the gleaming,
Moonbeams on thy bright hair streaming
      In the midnight-cold.

Closed on earth thy brown eyes' brightness,
Still lips frozen in their whiteness,
      Dust upon thy brow.
Far from Hartland thou art sleeping,
Stars above thee vigil keeping,
      Watching, we, below.

Grander soul ne'er wore a fetter;
Parting words e'er braver, better,
      Rived a golden bond.
Through the night-time, ever gleaming
Beacon-like, those words are streaming
      In the dark beyond:—

"I will never more forget you,
  Come the sunshine or the shadow
      To our earthly way.

But my country! hear her pleading,
While her bravest sons are bleeding!
    Must not I obey?

"Though the voice of love has power
Strong to move me in this hour,
    Sterner will might bend.
Glorious spirits round me falling,
Willing sacrifices, calling,—
    '*God and right defend!*'"

Other hearts than ours are breaking
With their weary weight of aching—
    Daily doomed to die.
Others, too, will break to-morrow,
'Neath the crushing weight of sorrow,
    In the tempest nigh.

Soldier sleeping! God is with thee!
Through the night-time ever weary,
    Loved ones far away
Wait *the reveille* at morning.
We shall greet thee in the dawning
    Of a brighter day.

TO A FRIEND,

ON RECEIPT OF SOME CURRANT-WINE.

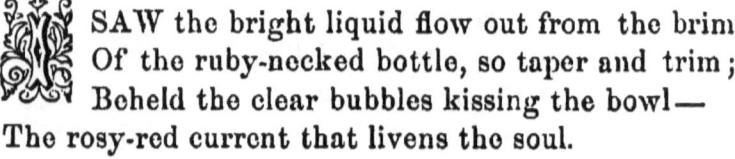 SAW the bright liquid flow out from the brim
Of the ruby-necked bottle, so taper and trim;
Beheld the clear bubbles kissing the bowl —
The rosy-red current that livens the soul.

Then tasting! and gently closing my eyes, —
I saw distant waves in their roseate rise, —
'Mid visions of yore — of the famous Rhine-land,
Where rich, purple clusters hung low on the strand.

'T was sweet as the nectar the honey-bee sips,
'T was red as the roses on beauty's soft lips,
'T was sparkling and bright as the dew of the morn
Whence glorious rainbows of noonday are born.

'T was a mystical draught, dear friend, I assure,
Limpid as constancy, steadfast and pure;
Fragrant as odors distilled from the flowers;
Enduring and strong as this friendship of ours.

PROMISE.

A LITTLE ring—a band of gold,
A circling, shining gift of old.
Frail symbol! what a wealth you hold
Of treasure never bought or sold;
Spring-blossoms lying 'neath the mould
Of time; *and heart that loved, grown cold.*

Ah! loved birds, joyous in the spring,
When autumn came, refused to sing;
Yet still I wear you, little ring,
A cold, bright, senseless, silent thing,
That binds me to the tears you bring,
And girds the cross to which I cling.

Ah! little ring, within your spell,
Was I those tides of soul to quell,
When listening to the golden bell
That rung the pæan? I loved too well,—
To dream how soon those chimes would knell
The loss and changes since befell.

Oh! rayless days that wail and pine,
All flowerless within the shine
And glory of an olden shrine
Of worship, that was too divine
With blossoms of the earth to twine.
Idolatry, thy curse was mine!

When toiling up fate's rugged steep,
And shadows to the summit creep,
The chimes bid me bend low to weep
For other years and hopes that sleep
Beneath life's outspread sunless deep;
I will fore'er my symbol keep,—
Till Christ those promise gates shall ope,
Where grows in realms of boundless scope
That border on life's sunset-slope,
The fruitage of earth's wasted hope.

TO S. A. H.

WHEN I, with listening heart, among
The spirits of that brilliant throng,
Heard first thy voice's witching trill,
And felt my inmost being thrill
With the sweet magic of each strain,
So blended in the rich refrain,—
It was as if some angel bright
Had blessed me with a new delight;
While I in turn could only bow,
And weave a chaplet for thy brow,
The brightest in the fair bright throng,
And, crowning, hail thee Queen of Song!

A glorious gift to thee was given.
The language of the saints in heaven

Could not be sweeter than the strains
Of music such as thy refrains,
Which linger long beyond the hour,
In cadences of wondrous power.
A charm — a memory — a spell —
A wish and prayer for thee. *Farewell.*

SUNRISE.

BEHOLD! o'er the steeps of the day,
Where the mist lies solemn and gray,
He cometh, the king of the morn!
With an amulet fair to adorn,
And to clothe the dim chaos of old
In verdure bespangled with gold;
And his armor is dimless and bright,
As when God said, "Let there be light."
Nature hails him with clarion-voice,
And the hearts of her people rejoice.

God's noblest creation is man!
The heart of his wonderful plan,
The soul for which deity died,
A creature divinely allied.

Through the waning light poor wandering feet
Tread slowly the pave of a broad still street,

As the wheels of time, with muffled tread,
Bear the hooded day to his twilight-bed.
"He is not old yet, the race half run
Holds sceptres merit alone has won
In the toil for gold, and the strife for fame,
And the sordid weight of an empty name."

Pale watcher, with faith growing faint,
With forbearance season thy plaint.
Great heart of humanity, sing
Of tidings the sunrise shall bring.

Let spirit-feet of a bygone time
Walk through life's night to its starry chime,
And find sweet joy in the weary round;
For love lived on, though the sun went down.

There's a glory still in the upper air,
And a world of wealth lies hidden there.
The radiance of Jehovah's smile
Will soon time's darksome glooms beguile,
Which circle above yon western gate,
Like the minions of resistless fate,
Whose messages are sounding knells
Rung by hope's twilight vesper-bells.

Far worlds in the spaces rejoice!
Ring into the chorus each voice;
God's glory the universe spans,
And the sun is the work of his hands.

HOPE IN DEATH.

TOIL on, toil on, through sunless days,
   O'er plains where shadows darkling lie;
   O heart, for thee drear desert ways,
  Through earth, and wail, and fear, and sigh,
For morning breaking o'er a maze
Of sunlit shores beyond the sky.
Life-bound, with but a fleeting breath,
And thine the entrance-gate, O death,
   To boundless life on high!

On gory fields our heroes fall;
   (O night of strife without a star;)
Uprisen at the country's call,
   Looking to God beyond the war.
At last enwrapt within thy pall,
   Which friend and foe so calmly wear,
When all is over, don thy wreath,
Descend thy rugged vales, O death,
   Close clinging to hope's spar.

As morning-suns light up the skies,
   And shine upon the battle-plain;
As stars that in the darkness rise,
   On ghastly faces of the slain;

Trusting, a bleeding nation tries
　　To win its way to peace again,
Through thee, thou victor, gloomy death;
With shroud and pall and cypress-wreath,
　　In hope we reign.

Though human voice has never stayed
　　The tides of death that round us roll,
No tomb that mortal hands e'er made
　　Can hide the grandeur of a soul.
In glorious spirit-form array'd,
　　Freed from earth's bondage and control,
Thou, heart, shalt greet the morn again
Of peace. And every hero slain
　　Has Christ's parole.

MY DREAM.

ALL the canopy of twilight,
　　Gathered with a golden thread,
　　Caught, as by a shining anchor,
In the darkness overhead;
Where grim, fitful shadows hovered,
　　And the stars gleam'd far and cold;
Mosses crisp the upland covered,
　　Mists lay thickly on the wold.

All without was rest and silence,
　　All within was seething pain;

And my head upon its pillow
  Dropt in weariness again.
I had seen the golden brightness
  Paling on the brow of night;
I had felt the cold stars glimmer
  On the home-bound track of light.

I had wandered over deserts,
  Wastes of arid, burning sands,
With no drop to cool the fever
  In my heart or wasted hands.
As I lay, so mutely waiting;
  Then the rustle of bright wings,
And such soothing strains of music,
  Bore me from all earthly things.

Ah! the world lay far behind me,
  I forgot my toil and pain,
And time's grieving billows o'er me
  Did not seem to surge again;
After I had caught the glimmer
  Of bright ocean's crystal clear,
Where I purged my earth-worn semblance
  From all traces of its fear.

Was it over — all my waiting,
  All my striving here below;
Wrestling with the forms of evil,
  Warring with the shapes of woe;
With so few to understand me,
  Or to read my freeborn soul:

Were, indeed, the fetters severed
   With the " breaking of the bowl " ?

Ah ! it was no dream — the flashing
   Of those golden wings was real;
And the gliding of the angels,
   With soft whispers of appeal,
Seemed to say again, " 'T is ended ;
   All life's sounds of pain and woe
With sweet triumph shall be blended :
   Wherefore dost thou linger so ? "

Then, beside the shining anchor,
   Burning clear upon the night,
There I saw another anchor —
   One small face, so wan and white,
In its weight of mortal anguish.
   Ah ! my heart grew hushed and still
While my earthly darling soothed me
   With her voice's wailing trill.

As she sung, the waiting serapns,
   Backward o'er the track of light,
Softly seemed to glide, and leave me
   With my loved one and the night.
Still she waited there beside me,
   When the morning, calm and slow,
Broke above the eastern gateway,
   Where our mornings come and go.

Then a cloud of sudden glory
   Trailed its brightness in our home ;

And a voice of mystic sweetness
  Echoed 'neath the arching dome:
Blent with prayerful thanksgiving
  That my life was mine again, —
And drear orphanage was spared her,
  With its loneliness and pain.

Better all my strife with living,
  Better toil and gloom and care,
Than to leave her, yearning, stricken,
  In a world so falsely fair;
Then my seraphs did not need me!
  Though my earthly darling clung—
To the heart that only listened
  To their music while she sung.

They were angels with the Father;
  We were pilgrims here below;
Yet it was his will we lingered
  On the thorny way of woe.
Sometime, as she sits beside me,
  Till the stars shall fainter gleam,
When bright anchors hold the darkness,
  I shall tell her of my dream.

LATONA.

A FACE looks through my sombre dreams to-
    night,
  With contour softened by an inner light,
Whereon my fancy cannot fail to trace
The proud soul's pure ideal — of winning grace,
And just the faintest touch of joy — to show
How blithe life's dreams, love-lighted, come and go.

The eyes meet mine with a keen flush of pain;
A sense of haunting harmony — a strain
Of spirit-melody; a pray'r — bygone:
Blent with a hope so sweet, so swiftly flown.
A nameless shadow on the high, pure brow,
An earnest want as I recall it now.

An aimless reaching out adown the years,
Through deserts darkened with the mist of tears,
For the soul's resting-place, — the better part
Of life, — the glad repose of heart to heart;
A voiceless yearning while the life-tides glow,
For many things the love-less cannot know.

Then there are other footprints on that face,
Of toil and conflict many a time and place;
The seething of still fires, which, day by day,
Consume the soul, or blight the form of clay.

The stolid bearing on through time's dull mart,
Of mortal ills that crush the waiting heart.

Though mines of unclaimed treasure lie between
The shining summit where the goal is seen ;
The unhewn pathway up time's giddy steep,
Where airy-footed phantoms dare not creep:
The heaven hangs very high, and hell below
With glories luring, and with fires aglow.

The soul a-wreck within the sight of home,
'Mid summers where the sunbeams never come ;
Or fire-flies glancing through the drowsy air,
Or troops of busy swallows hover there,
Beneath the shadow of a sombre pall,
That broods death-like within the silent hall.

No taper glows the blazing hearth to light
With Eden-gleam the palace-burdened sight ;
No earthly fane on which the mind is laid,
In the calm rest for which it yearned and prayed :
Only an inner temple with its stainless shrine,
And the sweet promise, "Soon shall home be thine."

"BEAUTIFUL SNOW."

AST by the bright wings of a seraph, the snow
From the uppermost heights to the earth
below:
Gently enwrapping a star-begemmed spread —
O'er homes of the living and graves of the dead.
Radiantly white, as the genii of story;
Pure as the saints in their robings of glory,
Whose soft tears of sympathy froze in their fall,
For the sin and curse that are over us all;
Fleecy and light from the olive-hued skies,
As the trailing insignia of paradise.
The one fair perishing thing that is given
To the world aglow with splendors of heaven.

Proud spirit! that told of the height whence you fell,
"Adown like the snow-flakes from heaven to hell."
God made you as fair as the beautiful snow;
He loves you, poor sinner, though you may not know
How deep in his Infinite heart sank your cry —
For shelter and rest of the crowd passing by,
Who spurned, and left you to die in the street,
With a bed and shroud of the snow and the sleet.
The world has cursed you, yet God has not said,
A soul shall be bartered for gold or for bread.

He knows all your erring and horrible woe!
The want and crime that have maddened you so.

All the dearer to him for strife and for stain,
And purer to-day for repentance and pain.
Made white by his blood as the beautiful snow,
"That falls on a sinner with nowhere to go;"
And sweeter the pardon hard-won by the cries
Which from Magdalen-lips went up to the skies.

O beautiful snow! from the filth of the earth,
Swift rising again in its cherubic mirth,
In crystalline dew-drops all glistening bright,
As clear, shining stars in a heaven of night.
If contrite to the throne of God's mercy we go,
He will lift up our souls like the beautiful snow.

ONE YEAR AGO.

A YEAR that came and went without its May
Or rosy June. This solemn, sunless day,
I think of one who went the silent way
To God's fair realm beyond. I heard the call
Which laid my heart's best self in shroud and pall,
Beneath last autumn's mould. Now red leaves fall,
And crisp and wither on a far-off bier.

O white-browed spirit, linger ever near
Unto my earth! I know thy soul is here;
I bow my head in dust, and muse of thee,
And of the many things that were to be.

Yet with the cold, cold sod on thy young breast,
Rude stranger-hands have laid thee to thy rest.
I see a pure white wreath whose blossoms die,
There is such autumn in the gale and sky.

One year of clinging darkness since has flown,
One year of waiting and of spirit-moan :
One year of battles lost and won on earth —
In whose still bosom he has slept. The hearth
By which I sit is desolate. Oh, stars above!
Sing ye the anthems of a deathless love,
Though other years stretch on as cold and gray
Their rounds of loneliness the life-long way.

In this sad autumn-time my spirit craves
Rest from the lashing of dark battle-waves.
Patience, tried heart! not yet. This may not be;
But in the nearing future thou shalt see,
The crimson channels closed, the nation free!
For faith has said so! dearly bought my trust —
He helped to fight this battle for the just.

Farewell, bright dream! weird shadows come and go
Before the stars, while cruel night-winds blow;
And flowers lie hidden 'neath the first pale snow.
A golden wave broke on the strand below.
The tides of life move on with sullen flow,
Without the hope that died one year ago.

OLD AND POOR.

OH! sexton, why do you toll the bell,
   Now Jeremy Benham is no more,
  In that careless way which says, "All's well;
'T is only a stranger old and poor"?

Too true! he was very old and frail;
  His scattered hair was crisp and white;
His life went out with a soundless wail,
  And his eyes had lost their joyous light —

So long ago! — Shall I tell you why,
  With God above, and his world around,
He was left alone in age to die,
  And his grave made in the "potter's ground"?

'T is a hard fate to be old and poor!
  I knew when Benham was rich and young;
And children three played 'round his door,
  'Mid vineyards where purple clusters hung.

I'll rehearse the tale! — yet bear along
  The stranger gone to his resting-place:
With a fetter cold on the limbs once strong,
  And morning-smile on the dead-white face.

OLD AND POOR.

His was a happy home — far away
    Where northern crags in the sunlight glow.
There's no blight on the land he loved, to-day,
    Though its countless hearts have felt the throe —

Of gushing death-tides every place.
    From arctic lines to antarctic shore,
There are pale tracks on many a face,
    And many wanderers old and poor.

'Neath a broken arch alone I stand,
    Grim ruin around me everywhere;
And the dun waves press from palms of sand
    Their names who, dying, traced them there.

Fair sun of the south, on barren ways —
    Beaten, bleared, and tracked with gore —
Thou gildest plains all seamed with graves,
    And the temple-shrines mock homeless poor.

Pass Benham by — let him rest. Adorn
    With a marble crest yon kindred grave.
His God will find him some sudden morn.
    Well I know his dying eyes did crave —

One more look at his boys. When the flame
    Burned low on his hearth — he was so old
To go abroad with his failing frame
    And homeless heart. Now his story's told.

His boys lie somewhere under the sod,
   In a winding-sheet of the blue they wore,
And Jeremy Benham — claim him, God! —
   Found dead, alas! on a prison-floor.

. . . . . .

Behold! yon glittering arch afar
   Spans temples of everlasting light.
The old and the poor are sheltered there,
   In heaven's home of the homeless. Bright

Are smiles of greeting — a white-robed form —
   A world of welcome in starry eyes —
To the jasper palace, fair and warm,
   And joy of the alien's paradise.

Ah! merrily clang your careless bell,
   For the old man's soul has found release;
He passed from yonder prison-cell,
   Through pearly gates, to eternal peace.

SACRIFICE.

ONLY another wreck,
   Heart, in thy silent deep,
   Where solemn soul-tides break,
And stars of memory weep.

Only another tomb
  On life's dumb-beaten shore;
Only gathering gloom
  Where glory flashed before.

Only a dark eclipse
  Hiding the sun of God;
Only two pallid lips
  Pressing the smiter's rod.

Very mute and cold and still,
  Curbing the restless plaint;
Of firm, undaunted will,
  With spirit sore and faint:

Anon two patient eyes —
  Uplifted through God's grace,
In faith to morning-skies
  Lit by the Saviour's face.

SPRING.

FROM towering height of glacier-dome
  Streams a pennon white of polar gloom
  Over the dun of the reaching hills,
And a leaden maze the chill air fills;
Though tides flow in from a dreary sea,
Bearing the arc of a spring to be.

SPRING.

With weary and laggard step she comes—
    Trailing the robes of winter after,
Along time's checkered isles where tombs
    Gleam white beneath her mocking sceptre.
While her voice rings out in sad surprise,
And the light pales in her sunny eyes,
As she views the earth so cold and dumb,
Giving no ear to the tidal hum,
With its frozen heart and silent voice,
Though the sylvan train bids it rejoice;
And spirits of the flowers bygone
Have crossed its slumber one by one. .
Loud echoes too of the thunder deep
Have shook the calms of its dreamless sleep.
As hushed and low—with pallid trace
Of icy death on its dun, wan face—
Lies still, though floods of the upper skies
Have drenched it with their sudden rise.
Poor planet of God!—a seal of fate
Has stilled thy pulse of spring in wait.

Poor, patient flowers under the mould,
Wooed by one beam of the springs of old,
And light of sun in the mazy air;
Ah! ye would not lie so dreamless there,
Awed by the tones of the thunder grand,
And thrilling touch of the lightning-wand.

Gentle forms we love lie hid to-day,
Low as the fairest flowers of May,

Waiting the touch of a mighty hand
To bid them rise with the voiceless band,
In stature of beauty more serene
Than our shrouded eyes have ever seen,
Whose radiant-like earth cannot hold
Nor dim. Neither flood, nor chill, nor mould,
Nor frozen heart of the world beneath,
Can a hope or heritage bequeath
Akin to the faintest bliss they know,
Where the springs immortal come and go,
With their living green and tides so bright,
Coursing o'er plains of lasting light,
Where love's sweet flowers of tender grace
Pale 'neath one beam from the Giver's face.

FOUR YEARS OF WAR.

LITHE, gliding swift from snow to snow again;
They passed, to join the melancholy train
Of things that were and are not. But compressed
In every breath an age of glory blazed!
An age of fear, with terrors wild amazed,
And world-old tale of crime; expired, redressed:
Forgiven to penitential will and main,
And to the plunging sacrificial pain,
Prolonged from Sumter. There the stars upon
Our flag grew dim, and sudden fell apart!

And gloom barbaric rushed our sky athwart,
E'en in the beauty of our glorious dawn:
Until our heroes' souls their light did pour
Into the paling stars, and, conquering, won
Them back to the blue field for evermore.

For swift the bugle's wild and liquid peal,
The tramp of armies, and the clash of steel,
A rayless darkness, and a quaking earth,
Began the process of our perfect birth.

Four years did then our banner trail in blood.
Four years death o'er the prostrate nation stood,
And clutched with bony hand her faltering heart.
Then plucked his banded skeletons—our flowers,
And broke our hearth-stones! taking all of ours
From which 'tis agony of soul to part.
Then every woe and every blight befell!
A chaos wild of hate! a carnival
Of murder and wide ruin; the red plain
Groaning beneath its hecatombs of slain.
Then, then broke first the bondman's world-long
    chain,
And smiles of victory, and the light of peace,
Came with deliverance from the Father's face.
No more we pine, or grieve, or fear; no more,
Thank God! we hear the thunder crashing fall
Of cities, faint no more at human gore.
No more we read the fearful lists of dead,
No more we tremble at the foeman's tread.

F

Yet many wounds our bruisèd spirits wear,
And there are vacant spaces everywhere;
Where mild bereavement holy shrines hath made,
For patient and eternal grief. The blade
Which sought our Chief's great heart had others found;
And from pale, dying lips there came a sound
Of mortal anguish. Their heroic pain;
Their loves and longings for themselves were vain.
Black robes, white faces, the sad story tell,
How they enjoyed not what they won so well: —
Though a world weeps that e'er this day they fell.
They passed the portal to *God's peace*, instead
Of this, their strong right arms have open spread
To us. Heirs of the blood-bought victory,
Whose sun, uprisen, lights their gory bed.
All silently they sleep beneath — while we
Enjoy our heritage of liberty.

IN THE SHADOW.

COME, draw the curtain softly, little one,
    And lay thy hand upon my burning brow;
  Let no fierce gleaming of the winter-sun
Fall red athwart my pensive dreaming now.

Come, dearie, sit beside me — closer yet;
  For many visions fill my aching head

Of those who journeyed with us. With regret
   I muse; for some are changed, and others dead;

Dead, like the old year, in storm, gust, and chill;
   As the fair, bright-browed summer gone before.
I hear the voices whose faint echoes trill
   Through my sad yearning heart for evermore.

Old winter, too, has laid him down to sleep
   In summer's grave, amid sere woodland ways.
I feel a shiver through my lattice creep,
   Spring's white-winged herald of her sunny days.

The snow lies on the young flowers — Pensee dear,
   And the cold March-sod upon her breast.
Four summers thou and I, so lonely here,
   Have lingered on, since sister went to rest —

Sleep, dream, in that bright, far-off home above.
   Yet in our hearts more palpable has grown
The semblance of our angel's deathless love —
   Love for two pilgrims roaming earth alone.

Alone? yes, in the shadow — all alone.
   The strong stay failed us when we gave our trust;
The tender care is from us, Pensee — flown;
   Affection withered; and 't is now but dust.

The dream is over — all, save memory, fled —
   Passed, as the summer from her woodland ways.
Abroad the day, with winter-sunshine red,
   The sun that wrapped us, Pensee, in his rays —

So brightly, dearie, in that long-gone time,
  Before it left us. All was darkness then.
We thought the world was chang'd, and joy's chime
  With thousand voices ne'er would ring again.

Away with dreaming now, for weary care
  Lies heavily upon my aching brain.
Yet thy dear dainty feet, my Pensee fair,
  Trip lightly to the tune of work or pain.

We are alone; yet strong are truth and right,
  And we will help each other to the end.
And One will help us whose great love is might!
  He aideth those who have no nearer friend.

Then put aside the curtain, Pensee dear,
  And let the broad, bright sunlight of God's love
Light our lone way through earth in quiet cheer,
  And lead us safely to her home above.

EVAN CASTLE.

EVAN CASTLE — old and gray!
  Moss-grown where the bright beams play
    Slyly through the dreamy summer.
Still the birds sing cheerily
O'er the silent manor-way.
  There they greeted many a comer

To the ruined homestead old;
For the lordly swains were bold.
   Lady Alice was so pretty,
Fair as flowers on the wold!
Nut-brown hair with hidden gold,
   Starry eyes with lashes jetty,—

Heaven's own blue! They closed, alas!
Though hot tears fell thick and fast.
   Oh! the drear dark flowing river,
Surging, dashing, driving past;
While they took one kiss — the last,
   And resigned her to the Giver.

Oh, the flashing autumn-morn!
Glinting o'er the waving corn,
   As we listen to the sighing
Of the wind o'er meadows shorn;
Hear the huntsman's distant horn,
   On his track crushed flowers lying.

And the crisp leaves flutter down,
Gold and purple, red and brown;
   Summer's rainbow-tints outvying.
Mist above yon busy town,
Castle-gate with ivy-crown,
   Drooping, faded, sere, and dying.

Starlight on the castle-floor,
Thou hast nestled here before
   In the sombre gloom so cheerless.

Night came through the open door.
She will come again no more
   Through the darkness bright and peerless.

Moonbeam lying there so white,
Like her spirit in the night;
   Pennon of the lost day's banner;
Footprint of the infinite!
Resting where the amber light
   Faded from the westland manor.

CASTE.

DOWN the unlighted vaults of time's dead years
   Peals the dull echo of unworded fears;
   Terrors of thee—unvanquished vampire—thou
Ruler of worlds! with bold imperious brow,
And golden sceptre in thy soft white hand;
Thy robe is purple, and iron thy wand.
Thy tones are mellow as the silver words
Of voices that proclaim thee "lord of lords."
Thy realm is earthwide, kings thy tools;
Thy dynasties the sporting mart of fools.

They do not always reap who till the soil,
And dullards snatch the prize from hands of toil.
Slothful patrician brows are laurel-prest,
When studious peasant learned the lesson best.

And seers have buried richer gems unseen
Than those which crown the sage's brow, I ween.
Genius must feed on husks, while idiots hold
The secret mine of many a miser's gold.
Truth, when the world was new, was christened
    great;
For something less than truth the ages wait.

The seas are still and deep as human souls!
Small rivers babble when their channel-holds
Cascade lithe as a gymnast — leaping down
Some dark abyss with avalanchine bound,
And dash of nature's chivalry, anon —
The eddy sinks in sand, the wonder's gone.
Though oceans hold their boast through countless
    years;
The fall of empires, and the people's tears.

Thou hast forged chains for eagle-souls to wear,
And wedded patient hope to blank despair.
Hast dwarfed and ruined many a noble aim,
Strangled the aspirant without *a name*,
Whose genius would have shaken thrones to reach
The privilege, the power, the gold of speech; —
Whose might had broken down a wall of craft —
To strike a tyrant with unerring shaft.
Thou hast polluted court and church and state;
Doomed Lazarus to die of want, at Dives' gate.

Earth's patriot-braves are ever first to fall,
Because the last to shrink from death or pall.

Life's highest honors are blood-bought of worth!
Through thee, the poltroon wears a cloak of birth —
And braggart steals the hero's wreath. The slave
Of base desire fills oft a lordling's grave.
The feckless piety unknown to test,
Is ever voted purity — the best,
Though perjur'd before God — besotted — lost
The soul in Stygian pools the body cross'd.
While some lealer spirit has fallen low
Down where perdition's black tides ebb and flow.
Thou too shalt perish in the quenchless fire,
When world on world shall light God's altar-pyre.
With every false, fair thing consumed at last,
Thou blasting scourge, thy sleek-tongued demon,
  Caste!

ON A PORTRAIT.

  RAPT angelic one!
  I love to gaze upon thy sainted face,
  With features of inimitable grace,
And contour of exquisite loveliness:
  My beautiful, my own!

  O lips so ripe and rare!
 So sweetly parted, as if to say
 In thine own lisping, childish way,
 "Mamma, I love you all 'e day,"
  And smile serenely fair.

ON A PORTRAIT.

O brow so clear and high!
Pure with white radiance shining o'er,
Shadowed with bright waves of golden hair;
Whose tints remind us of the summers where
    Our loved one's never die.

More wondrous still than all —
Thy gentle eyes, clear shining as a star,
Whose beams by love so sweetly chastened are;
Whose mystic splendor neither life could mar,
    Nor death, nor grave, nor pall.

Earth was too drear a place,
For thee who wert so lovely, pure, and good.
Alma, we would not, even if we could,
Have kept thee, darling, from the angelhood.
    Behold! upon thy face —

The glory thou dost share.
My angel on the earth, now God's and mine,
Gone with hosts of the redeemed to shine,
Yet with radiance never more divine,
    Or shape more sweetly fair,

Than that which beams on me,
Wearing the charm thy living beauty wore;
The spirit-impress which it early bore;
The heav'nly cast thy Saviour sent before
    Earnest of what should be.

HIDDEN AWAY.

THERE are pure beams from the upper day,
Hidden from sight in our forms of clay.
A glory-gleam from the world of stars,
Illumines shapes the spirit wears,
Whose chords are swept by a hand divine,
Whose flowers lie fadeless on love's shrine.

Though the world moves staidly on and on,
And the rack of life be meekly borne,
Its tasks wrought out with throbbing brain,
Its ascents spanned with heaving pain,
Its toils endured with patient grace
That the flitting days may leave no trace
On the inner life so deep and true:
And the seals remain unbroken too.

Hidden away in the soul's bright deep,
Where the fullest tides of being sleep,—
There are mystic voices, low and grand!
The sweet refrain of a spirit-band;
The undertones of the surging sea,
Of passion bound and hope set free,
Held in the clasp of finite will.
Fathoms down 'neath the surface still,
Dwell the burning dreams we cannot tell;
Deep in the heart's dim, silent well.

We hear a voice from the pristine deeps,
Where the spirit's brightest semblance sleeps,
And mystic strains from the music sweet
Where the silver stars and sunbeams meet:
We feel a pulse in the waiting heart
Thrill to its blessèd counterpart:
The shadowy clasp of a loving hand
Which sways our being at command;
A spirit-touch from the pure, sweet lips,
Whose tints the morn's bright hues eclipse.
Behold a flash of the wild, vain dream,
Whose hallowed sun with lightest beam,
Would make all life a blest reward.
Yet from the heart's unbroken sward,
Earth crushes the spirit's brightest bloom,
'Neath the iron tread of fate and doom.
We work and wait through life's toilsome night
For the goal disclosed to mortal sight,
With the glow of Eden in our stars.
For the moving slow of crystal bars,
Dividing us from the world above
Of the soul's pure life—*whose law is love.*

A PRAYER.

FATHER! on thy name I call,
  My way lies hid in night;
And darkness, like a sombre pall,
  Has shut thee from my sight.

My path is bleared with human tears —
   And doubt, and groan, and cry;
While I, borne down with mortal fears,
   Beg that this cup pass by.

The crown of thorns is pressing sore,
   The sword has pierced my side;
I drag the cross that Jesus bore;
   O Master! be my guide;

And deign to let thy great love shine
   Upon my shrouded way;
Oh! may thy tender eyes divine
   Beam on me while I pray.

Grant me, dear Lord, the boon I crave!
   In humbleness I bow
Before thee. O my Saviour! save
   Me — or I perish now.

ARION.

WHERE my love-star sank in gloom,
   High, bright gates of morning loom.
Memory lights affection's tomb
When anew the lilacs bloom.

ARION.

Flowers spring on gilded plains.
    Bounds the life-tide through my veins!
Melts the past in tearful rains,
    Musing of the rosy chains—

Woven in the long-ago.
    But the glory faded slow,
In a spring whose crystal flow
    Broke in murmurs soft and low—

O'er the path we jointly trod!
    Greenly grows the April-sod.
Spirit bowing 'neath his rod,
    Mounts the starry way to God.

Footprints 'neath a desert sun,
    Where no crystal rivers run;
Over meadows crisp and dun,
    Lies my life-track, Arion.

Other springs, their glories shine,
    Flower and garland, bower and vine.
While their low winds wail and pine,
    Thinkest thou of me and mine?

In thy altered fate and way,
    Wheresoe'er thy feet may stray;
Whether 'mid the grave or gay,
    Wilt thou live again the day—

When my young heart gave to thee
    All its wealth and melody.

Oh! the songs we sung in glee,
  Sitting 'neath the gilead-tree.

Warming meadows, crisp and dun,
  Golden gloams the west'ring sun
When the far, bright goal is won,
  I shall meet thee, Arion.

LIGHT AND DARKNESS.

OH, there are hours in which we live a life
So fleeting and yet so intense, it seems
As if an age had crept into the span:
Belting the brief, bright space with messages,
That fell upon the thirsty soul like dew
On flowers crisp, or raindrops crystal-clear—
Upon the arid deserts of our way.

Oh! there are dreams — too holy, too divine
For even dreams to be in this cold sphere
Of withering reality. Must we,
Then, lay our lips in dust and humbly say,
"I'll try to trust" — though blindly, prayerlessly.
"Let this go by. My God, oh, strengthen me
To learn that lesson conned by sons of men,
Of faith so sweet, and yet so hardly won —
' Thy everlasting will — not mine — be done.'"

LIGHT AND DARKNESS.

Oh, there are moments when the holy calm
Of some tried spirit wafts its toil-won peace
Over the barren wastes of some poor heart
That hungered, thirsted, yet strove in vain,
Fainting 'neath scorching suns, to purge and bless,
Like palm and oasis of living green;
And fruits of righteousness, above the pass
'Twixt effort and achievement; tempting him
To one last effort for the goal that lies
Anear to heav'n and immortality.

There is a madness, subtle and intense,
As the wild delirium of brain or sense —
A fantasy of soul — a reaching vain
Of spirit-wings aloft — a wordless pain —
A rack of torture, and a cry for light,
Seeking in Lethe's maze a gloom made bright.

Oh! I have traced, on many a human face,
The majesty of truth denied — and faith,
And all the grace of higher things! and hope
Wrecked ne'er on mortal sea of blinding tears.
Bright shapes, though clad in sombre hue, were near,
As if to guard and cherish such, though life
Wore but the simple guise of duty done.

Life once had been to them a struggle rife
With passion-haunted dreams, and hours
Of waking, when they strove and strove in vain;
To fail and fail again — as though the scale
Were held by hand of demon or of ghoul;

As if each day held only other tests
Of strength that could but fail, and hope
That ever paled in the vain search for rest.

Rest!—vain, delusive word! Who, though his soul
Were lifted high above the plains we press,
Can say, until the race is run, and time,
As now, has ceased to be, "*I have found rest*"?

Yet with this never-ending rack and round,
And routine unto which we're darkly bound;
Are there not some things nobler, better far
Than useless drifting with the surging tide,
Or steerless floating on an ocean wide
Of mortal life, immortal destiny?

Dare we lay idols broken and despoiled,
By sinful touch profaned, upon a shrine—
Worthy alone of purest homage? God's love
No longer shines upon us, though we weep
And lose our way amid the starless maze
Of shoreless dark, upon an unknown sea:
If we have ceased to supplicate for light!
The glory of the everlasting sun
Of righteousness by faith and prayer won.

NEVERMORE.

OUR school-time is done!
A new life has begun,
With bright hopes and dark fears
For the swift coming years:
 Free from tears —
  Nevermore.

The parting has come!
Each will go to her home,
Other loved ones to greet,
And perchance we shall meet
 Here again
  Nevermore.

The old bell shall peal
For our woe or our weal;
Like a voice from above,
Breathing sadness or love:
 Still for us
  Nevermore.

Ah! happy mates, when
We are women and men;
With the harrowing cares
That maturity bears,
 And are gay
  Nevermore!

When years have gone by,
We will tell with a sigh,
Of the hearts that grow cold —
And their love-treasures hold
   "As of old,"
     Nevermore.

Each still summer-morn
We'll recall what is gone;
And the faces divine,
Making other days shine
   That will shine
     Nevermore.

And autumn will moan
O'er the days that are flown;
And the waves on the shore,
Breaking gayly before,
   Will repeat,
     "Nevermore."

In summers to come!
May we meet in God's home —
Teachers, pupils, and friends,
Where the term never ends.
   There to part —
     Nevermore.

WILLIE LEE.

SWIFT coursing through Eden, a dark river ran,
Blighting love-flowers that grew on its beautiful strand,
As it swept on and on to the port that we see,
Where Christ anchored the bark of our fair Willie Lee;
When we laid his dear form 'neath the willows to rest,
And his soul tried its wings in a realm of the blest.

Mother's heart was his pillow, when roses were new,
And the sweet meadow-lilies oped petals of blue.
But the daisies are faded, the grasses grown sere
On the footprints of spring-time, since Willie was here.
Oh! the sun of September shines mournfully now,
The dust of the valley has kissed his bright brow.

The golden-haired pet of the household was he;
Ah! the fairest and brightest, our dear Willie Lee.
There are lines growing deep on the kind father's brow.
And the mother! her heart is sore broken now.
At morning, at noontime, at evening, at night,
She will miss what September has hid from her sight.

She will hear the waves murmur that bore him away.
Praying e'er for the light of the beautiful day—
That is his — on her path : and will tearfully keep
Tireless watch through the night on the shore where
    we weep.
Till the fanes of the Lord shall rise from the deep,
And she rests where they laid Willie Lee down to
    sleep.

IN MEMORIAM.

OH! would that any little word of mine,
  Could still your craving vain,
    Or give the treasur'd shape, for which you
      pine,
  To your fond arms again;—

Or wake the tender tones that now are still,
  Whose music low and deep,
Was soft and witching as a summer rill,
  That sings itself to sleep.

Then were it well to speak; but now, oh, no!
  The footprints are yet warm,
Your dear one left upon the world below,
  And passed beyond the storm.

Yet with caressing lingers ever here,
   With timid heart so fond;
And that loved face is shining sweetly near,
   The border line beyond.

But I can tell you how I feel your pain,
   And hold your sorrow mine;
And breathe a hope that you may clasp again,
   That spirit form — divine,—

Beyond the confines of this weary earth,—
   Beyond death's rolling tide:
Within the area of immortal birth,
   Where fate nor woe divide,—

Us from the shapes we wildly worship still,
   E'en while we kiss the rod,
And bow before the everlasting will
   Of an all-gracious God.

THE FEMALE PHARISEE'S SOLILOQUY.

OH, once I loved you, poor, unhappy friend!
   Now, though you need me, I abandon you.
   My course and policy I must defend,—
The autocratic world has censured you.

It failed to understand you; hence it blamed.
   'T is easy to conceive a wrong, we know;
'T is right to turn away from one defamed
   By the most blighting curse that follows woe.

True, we have some attributes in common —
   A kindred love and pride, to which we bow.
Though I am saintly — *you are only woman;*
   And God has made me " holier than thou."

Scourged by life's sorry ailments, I was born
   To wear pure vestments, and ignore the stain
Of what would make me "*nervous;*" though the scorn
   I feel for you, is greater than my pain.

My heart is tender — swift to know a wrong;
   Your waywardness afflicts me as a blow.
Why will you shock me, when you should be strong
   To bear the burden that is crushing slow?

My narrow sphere is kindly made for me,
   By loving hands as sunny as the May.
Your desert is world-wide — a upas-tree
   Has cast its shadows on the weary way.

Each want anticipated ere I call —
   'T is given me to dream the summer through.
Your task it is to strive; and, rise or fall,
   'T is easier to doubt you than be true.

Here, in the sunlight of my happy home,
   I coldly scan your poverty and pain.

THE FEMALE PHARISEE'S SOLILOQUY.

I shar'd your brighter days; yet have you come
   To see life's harvest ripen — fall — in vain.

I turn away in doubt, and wrap around
   My form the stainless vesture of my pride.
I'm forced to "cut" you, as in "duty bound,"
   I wear a symbol of the justified.

What matter though your feet are bleeding, sore,
   Blistered, galled with arid, burning sands;
True, I might bathe them, as in days of yore,
   And bind your broken heart with kindly hands.

One word would take the envenom'd sting
   Of keen injustice which your spirit cow'd,
And from love's fount sweet compensation bring.
   A God on earth beneath your weight was bow'd.

He knew the way and warfare would be hard.
   "Judge not," he said, "but I command ye, love
One another." Yet for this you're barred
   From e'en the hope of bliss with Christ above.

How "*Jesus wept*" when at the grave of friend
   He saw the death-cold body hid away;
Praying the Father might his Spirit send
   To light anew the temple of its clay.

I cannot weep, though I have seen you crave
   Some recognition of the far, bright past.
'*Twas Godlike to forgive; yet Heaven defend
   Me from such weakness, saintly to the last.*

THE FEMALE PHARISEE'S SOLILOQUY.

You trailed your drapery through the dusty street,
  Where sin ran riot in the noonday's light.
I turn my back upon you when we meet —
  I shut your phantom out into the night.

Why has God set you homeless in his dark,
  If you was worthy to enjoy my light?
There is a rendezvous for paupers — work!
    You must be strong, though you look worn and white.

The winds, like flaming voices round you howl!
  Is there no murmur on your faded lip?
Your face with want is seamed, yet wears no scowl;
  Despair has clutched you with a bony grip,

That leaves you wordless! Can an outcast pray,
  Stricken and cold within homelit street?
Ah! there is supplication in the gray
  Shade on your face, and in the look I meet.

Once, long ago, you prayed for me, when ill,
  You watched beside, I thought your faith so sweet.
The pleading earnestness was proudly still
  When I denied you in the crowded street.

Your eyes were dim and stony! though a light
  Seemed breaking through the fixed and rigid stare,
Which said: "Do you forsake me?" then the night
  Closed round more solemn when I left you there.

THE FEMALE PHARISEE'S SOLILOQUY.

Though in my inmost soul I could not doubt;
   Stricken you were, but pure I must believe;
Though there are none to search the problem out,
   A sullied reputation to retrieve.

Yet if you, scourged, are sinless, what am I,
   With home and hopes to make me better still?
Your judge, censor, executioner. Why
   Reverse the verdict of imperious will.

In my prolonged and ceaseless struggle rife
   With physical, exhausting pain — I thought
It easier to strive *with life* than *for life.*
   God's clemency is free! while man's is bought.

And then there is such proneness in the race,
   To trample down a soul with wrong assailed.
There is yet majesty in that wan face,
   I dare not gaze on, 't is the truth unveiled.

To your proud spirit blighting was my doubt:
   A blow — a clinging curse to bow you down;
Surer than destiny which shuts you out
   From happiness, from fortune, and renown;—

All that you bravely strove in vain to win!.
   Compelled the wild hope to abandon where
You were bewildered with the varying din
   And hush, and after numbness of despair.

Ah, well, you go your way; I'll cling to mine!
   Intrenched and happy, lend no helping hand

To rescue those who, maim'd, or halt, or blind,
   Are cast by fate's cold surges on time's strand;—

While over ocean-waters warm and wide,
   I ride the highest waves that ebb and flow.
Counting mad pulses of the storms — inside
   Life's freighted frigate, where the heart-lights glow.

Mayhap you'll starve or die, for aught I care:
   I'm not responsible. How the winds shriek!
The stars burn fainter in the gaslight's glare,
   The air is dim with swaying spectres bleak.

Was that a moan, or groan? It could not be
   That haunting look upon your face meant death!
Hark! hark! "*O Lord, have mercy upon me!*"
   She's dead! dead on the threshold of my wealth.

. . . .

Deny no longer I the outcast now;
   She so transformed with death's restoring touch.
The majesty of peace is on her brow,
   The impress of a love that suffered much:—

Was tortur'd grievously with doubt and pain!
   E'en betrayed in trusting to the last.
And yet that pale, calm sleeping shows no stain
   Of way or warfare in the conflict passed.

Who of her censors now would sooner die,
   Than take the wages of the world; or bow
Before want's dread necessities? Not I —
   Untried can say — "I'm holier than thou."

Yet holier than thou the world esteemed
   Many who knew not your heroic rise.
Poor dead! unclaimed — unworthy deemed.
   Was God ashamed to shelter with his skies?

His was the love you found when all was lost,
   And his the voice that bade you struggle on
To victory. He held the wave you crossed,
   And cradled you in peace, the battle won.

Oh! not too holy thou — great God of all,
   Thou heart of love — deliverer from sin!
To hear repentant sinners when they call
   To thee, " 'tis sweet to let the pardoned in."

FIFTEENTH KENTUCKY INFANTRY.

THERE'S a rise and fall as of many feet,
   And the muffled sound of the victor's drum;
A veteran throng in the morning street;
   The Fifteenth returning home!

True souls, amid anguished reaches dim,
   Ye have threaded a sacrifice profound,
While the torch of hope burned red and dim
   Afar on the slaughter-ground.

It is fearful to view those ranks again —
   So wasted, and think of another day;

And the many who come not back again,
    Though a thousand went away.

They were thinned and scourged, yet cut their way;
    With nerveless hands won the victor's crown,
And planted the standard of liberty —
    Where the good and brave went down.

While we bid thee, patriots, welcome home,
    We mourn for the valiant spirits fled,
Who passed from the battle's gory gloom
    To bivouac with the dead.

Though our gleaming banner streams on high,
    With the starry wealth of other years,
There's blood on its folds! — and the nation's sky
    Is dark with the mist of tears.

LITTLE PAUL.

'TWAS night o'er the world, yet morning-bells
    Chimed high in heaven's cupola —
The gleaming tips of the asphodels,
    Where fruits of life immortal grow —

The "bridge of flowers" o'er which he came,
    The "starry way" o'er which he passed.
All these I saw in a troubled dream —
    Then woke to the vacant space, alas!

LITTLE PAUL.

And the sunless day, so bleak and cold,
   With a mist of hot tears gloaming o'er
The tiny tracks on the summer-mould,
   Awoke, to hear his voice no more.

Cold are the lips we kissed at will,
And the baby-hands are folded, still,
On the little pulseless heart. Those eyes,
Vague with splendors of paradise,

Are closed. There are heads low-bowed,
   And a " bridge of flowers " hid with snow;
And the flaming white of a tiny shroud
   Lies over the " starry way," we know.

But there's a name on yon jasper wall —
Kind hands outstretched to welcome Paul;
And his baby-face is glowing bright,
In God's temple of eternal light.

That Father's smiting was rich with joy
   And promise. " *Of such my kingdom* " *fair*,
" *Let them come to me.*" Resign thy boy
   To the *Christ of little children there.*

10

THE DEAD LOVE.

LIFTING its spirit to God everywhere
   With pure trust.
 Bending its brow, the earth-fetters to wear,
Deigning its exquisite blisses to share.
Stricken to-day, lying peerless and fair —
   Low in the dust.

Its beautiful life — vanished and gone.
   Ah! we know,
It came with the rosiest tints of the dawn,
Seeking far vistas of earth to adorn;
Faded as flush from the face of the morn, —
   Stilly and slow.

A shape that was lovely: lay it to rest,
   'Neath the sod,
With hands mutely folded on the still breast,
Knowing how true lips the dead ones have pressed,
Trembling and pallid with inward unrest, —
   Kissing the rod

Of God's chastening. A grief-stricken trill,
   Rife with woe,
Runs the sacrifice through. Fate's measure fill
From a living heart broken, never to thrill
To the dead one lying, icy and still, —
   Buried low.

'Twas May — 'tis midwinter. Into life's gray
    Dips the sun.
Near a still, white corpse of the past alway,
E'er lingers a mourner, kneeling to pray,
Striving to teach her poor lips how to say —
    "Thy will be done."

DAISY-TIME.

WITH strange sweet tides our hearts run over,
    And joyous fulness almost pain.
    O'er meadows crisp of faded clover,
We cross to vistas of youth again, —

'Mid hawthorns wearing their icy garlands —
    Flashing stars in the air so still.
The snow-bird's pipe to the eagle soaring
    Beyond the range of their low, soft trill.

The spring lies locked in dreamful wonder,
    Fast asleep in the April-cold:
With the wealth of many seasons under,
    The calm expanse of silent mould.

PAST.

THE winds of winter are wailing low
O'er tombs of summers under the snow;
O'er whose pallid reach the sunbeams lie,
We dream of hours that are long gone by.

A school-time, merry and far away,
And tasks filling each gleesome day;
Life's daisy-dotted spring was fair,
Its halo in the April-air.

Daisies gemm'd the grass in shady nooks,
They were pressed between the leaves of books:
And rippled the waves of golden hair.
Daisies and sunshine were everywhere.

We wove bright wreaths on the smiling green;
And there were none fairer ever seen
Than the crowns we made of pure white sprays,
With calm of peace in the golden days.

PRESENT.

TURN to that bygone season mild,
And sigh for the merry-hearted child
Who carolled 'mid its sands as free,
As birds on the wing of minstrelsy.

There's a frail form on a desert strand,
Threading lonely ways at fate's command:
Through the earth's wide wastes!—eternity,
Will the border-land of sorrow be.

Then I think of the form so prized,
With his lofty mien and starry eyes;
And the bright hours of a sunny May,
When her young head on his bosom lay.

I hear no chant of the summer gone!
Its glory paled, its foliage strown.
His heart is so cold and far away,
It hears not the wail from hers to-day —

Nor sorrows — though many heedless feet
Trample her soul in the sad life-beat.
The faltering pace — the lonely ways,
Of a loveless woman's aimless days.

The home made bright as the smile of God,
With faces under the April-sod.

The first that died, and the grave we made,
Now nestled close 'neath the gilead-shade.

And the angel-guest of Christmas-time,
He loved her with a love sublime!
Yet her life, too, the Saviour claimed,
One chill March-day ere the daisies came.

When spring-dews glistened as of old,
And the May sun shed its molten gold
O'er wavy meadows — her summer-time
Had blossomed in a brighter clime.

Time, by the links of our hopes and fears,
Drags the iron chain of weary years;
From whose care-stain'd brow the fairy-crown,
By a hand beloved was stricken down.

Though the seasons swiftly come and go,
Daisies we love lie under the snow.
The home-light pal'd — and a stranger's face
Lights by-gone scenes in the first love's place.

FUTURE.

SURE daisies with dew-drops all ablaze,
In the starry gleam of other days,
Will flash in radiance, when we stand
By the judgment-bar, at God's command.

Then each shall know how much was lost,
In that reckoning long — the fearful cost.
If the pearls of love thus cast away,
Will gem the brow of the coming day;

Whose night hangs over our mortal sky —
When life's freighted ships at anchor lie,
On the river death, which stretches wide
Its sullen waves! On the farther side,

Bright doors of spring-time open stand!
A glory gleams on the golden strand;
And the daisies blossom fadeless there,
In the pearly sheen of upper air.

HILLS OF MAYSVILLE.

CHANGELESS, changeless hills!
Though motionless and still,
Ye stand beneath your sheet,
Of crustless, clinging snow.
Great hills, I love you so!
Old friends, ye were mine own;
My dearest, earliest known.
The brightest promise-bow —
My sky has ever bless'd,
Spann'd thy expanse — and best
Of hopes grew on thy crest.

Now as thine own my heart is cold,
'Neath frozen cover — hills of old.
My years like winter ripple on;
Though changeless stand ye — much is gone.
The echoes of the tones lov'd most,
Remain of all that summer's boast.

O prayerless, prayerless hills!
My soul its voice of worship stills,
To see you look so stern and grand —
Lapp'd close beneath the mighty hand,
That smote, and smote ye where you stand.
From age to age your summits rise
Still changeless to the changeful skies.

I am so awed as with my gaze,
On your vast reaches, — hidden ways
With gloom more sombre skirt my days.
It seems so strange to see you so;
Dead giants shrouded with the snow.
Whose record pure my heart has read,
On glacier-stone at foot and head.
God clothed ye once with verdure, and his voice
In lost love's human tones, bids me rejoice.
  He is my stay and strength forever true,
  All changeless — changeless like to you
  Great hills 'neath heaven's arching blue.

O heart, what fate can ever shut from thee
The radiance of this great infinity!
O hills, what snows of time can blight your crest,
Locked in the slumbers of eternal rest!

THE MOTHER'S LAMENT.

WHAT is it, darling mother? There's a shadow
    on your brow,
    And to all our merry sallies your voice is silent
    now.
The Christmas-hearth grows red, while the ruby wine
    is poured;
There are smiles upon the faces you love, around the
    board.

My child, far o'er the eastern hills the morn is break-
    ing cold,
Around their towering crags and trees that shiver,
    gray and old.
On bleak meadows, where in spring bright flowers are
    wont to grow,
Dark spirits of the storm have left their silver tracks
    of snow.

And the bare, crisp lowlands, dearie, look as they did
    one day;
And winter-thistles lift their heads from out the
    frozen clay—
Just as upon *that* morning; and the wind's sigh of
    unrest
Seems but the sob of sorrow hushed within my
    lonely breast,

Where a golden head was lying all through the summer long,
While bright-winged warblers carolled merry peals of song.
But the season with its flowers, as that spirit, passed away;
Doomed was the temple of our hearts to slow and sure decay.

Though many a Christmas morning has broken o'er the steeps
'Yond which he passed, I'll ne'er forget the little one, who sleeps
With a smile upon the baby-face we buried long ago,
And the roses on the waxen cheeks, now lying 'neath the snow.

It was a glance far brighter than the limpid shaft of dawn
Which pierced the jasper battlements of everlasting morn.
There's a voice whose tones are sweet as notes of the redeemed,
And a step like winter-fairy's on the meadow and the stream.

He joins the Christmas matinee, kneels at the Saviour's feet,
With a halo on his pure white brow, his hands in rapture meet.

The tiny hands we pressed, and the brow caressed
    at will.
Oh, our baby, though an angel now, is our baby still.

Through God the Christ, our Saviour — He who died
    that we might live:
He took our treasure from us, a more precious boon
    to give —
This hope — that when all seasons with their bright-
    est treasures pale,
We may claim a life immortal beyond the sunset vale.

A SONNET.

"NEARER and nearer," the cold drops say.
"Nearer the end of the toilsome way.
Nearer the point where the strife shall cease.
Nearer the plains of the perfect peace.
Nearer the harvest of time's great loss!
Nearer the pass where the two roads cross.
One leading up to the spirit's arc;
One bearing down through the unknown dark,
Through the valley of shadows cold and gray,
Till they blend anew in the upper day.
Nearer the close of the waiting night.
Nearer the morn in whose glorious light
Two souls life's current shall mingle free
In a tide of exultant ecstasy."

MAGGIE RAYMOND.

SONNET.

ALDRICH tells us of a " bridge of flowers,"
   By which come cherubs to this world of ours.
   Bright spirits from the higher realm of bliss,
Adown the starry stairway unto this.
All tremblingly thy untaught baby-feet,
Which very lightly pressed the golden street,
Came slowly o'er the narrow strait between
The lower world and that bright land unseen.
And from thy beauteous face so pure and fair
Looks forth the angel that was *missed up there*,
When thou wert found upon the home-bound track,
Astray, till mother-arms should bear thee back.
Thou, tiny messenger, to her wast given
To make the way more clear from earth to heaven.

"THE BLUE AND THE GRAY."

THROUGH our land a dark current is welling!
   Its cliff-ridden banks are o'erflown
   With fierce tides that are madly repelling
  The check which their calmness doth own.
Stretching on to the locks of a haven
   Where lieth a vessel in wait;

Though her crew are not coward or craven,
  They wear the steel armor of hate.

Hear them sing of disunion! that band,
Though unable to drift or to stand
'Neath the blight of a curse on the land.

    " Oh, thou tides slow and wide,
      Which our sections divide!
      Ye are fordless, and deep
      As the waters that sleep
        In the caves of the sea."

    Answer sprite, risen free
    From serfdom and thrall:
    " O thou God over all!
    Who hast cleft a strong chain
    Of the ages in twain;
    Thy bright crown lieth light
    On the brow of the right."

Yet that crew are dumb to the siren,
  Who chanteth her liquid refrain.
Shrill voices cry—" Give back the iron
  And steel of that lengthening chain!
Let it enter the soul, and environ
  The slave with his bondage again."

Then the waves gave for answer — " No, never!
The Master hath broken their chain;
And his edict for ever and ever,
Will peal through the ages amain."

TO MRS. S. V., OF PHILADELPHIA.

PATIENT and gentle, tender, kind, and true!
Thine is a life in which bright blossoms grow,
Of faith and righteousness. The test was hard,
Though hours of pain bring e'er a rich reward.
The rest at last will be for thee so sweet.
Thy burden meekly laid at Jesus' feet,
There 'll be no pain or woe in heaven we know,
In all the countless years that come and go,
Thou 'lt measure then the path which here was trod
And know, though thorny, it led up to God.

RECOMPENSE.

THROUGH many a sweet golden eventide,
Profoundly happy, I sat by your side,
You were the brightest sunbeam of my day!
Was it a dream? or did I hear you say, —
"Oh, never more, my dearest, grieve or pine:
My heart, my life, my hope, my soul, are thine."

When the vesper chimed the hour of prayer;
My pulses throbbing, told me — "he is near."

And when my form on bended knee sank low,
Our lives to wondrous oneness then would flow,
Toward that sea where time's swift rivers run,
Their course beneath the everlasting sun.

And when the parting came, and growing space
Hid from your eager eyes my form and face;
When your proud soul reel'd 'neath my last sad words,
And all your life was full of broken chords;
And all the light that would have made life blessed,
Like vanished suns shone only in the past; —

Then in the darkness when your strength gave way,
And you lay prostrate through the live-long day;
What were your thoughts throughout the solemn
  night,
When your soul panted for the coming light?
When you felt life and love were incomplete,
Till you had laid your world down at my feet.

Anon, "old Charon backward bore his boat."
Time on your heart a strange, sad lesson wrote.
It was the old, old contest, love and pride.
Youth, beauty, wealth, were on my rival's side.
Mine was a poor, plain face 'mid fashion's throng,
And then the world heard not the *soul that sung.*

Yet it was hard for you to turn from hours
Whose bliss and melody we counted ours.
From all the glory of the life we plan'd;
Where blue seas kiss a fair Provencian strand.

And fate and heaven wooing us to come,
And take the gift which God had given us, "*home.*"

We might have made life blest for others there.
The soil of mind, when pure, great fruits may bear.
Yet now those visions mock me, and I weep,
To know you guard her in her peaceful sleep —
Upon your heart, that fair young bride; and oh!
I long to lay *my head* beneath the snow,

When from the casement of my lonely room
I watch the autumn in its sombre gloom,
Grow dark with winter in the leaden sky,
And troops of browning leaves go flitting by.
I seem to kiss the sculptur'd lips so strange —
And cold beneath the clinging snows of change.
My earth, my heaven was the hope that's fled!
I mutely shiver while I bow my head.
Though faith has taught me that the souls above —
Who needs *must love* to live — will *live to love.*

―――――――――

THE GAY PALACE.

REARED aloft on Chestnut Street,
    Stands a palace fair and stately;
  Built of marble — quite complete —
With its splendid treasures lately —

THE GAY PALACE.

Brought from Nuremberg and Hyda,
Prague and Gottemburg, Vienna
And Berlin in costly manner.
O'er the surging of the water!
Boundless stores of terra-cotta
Came: and money has been spent
At Hanley, and Stoke upon Trent;
And such hosts of wonders sent
E'en from Birmingham and Breslin,
Rivalling a Turkish harem.
For such trains of ladies gather
In the cool, sunshiny weather,
Looking fair and bright as May,
In the palace of the Gay.
While yon marble Cupid strives,
With dart keen as Sheffield knives,
To engrave each pretty face
On the glass-ware and the place,
Like the demoiselles of Paris!
Whence were brought these toys—
Rarest, dearest little shapes of magic;
And the statues acting tragic—
Scenes amid medallion vases,
Studded with such antique faces.
All the splendors which we dream
Must a very mockery seem,
Here amid such dazzling glories,
Wonderful as fairy stories,
Where bright crystal fountains play,
As one grand tri-u-nity,
In the temple of the Gay.

11*

THE LAST ROSE-BUD.

ONE little frozen bud of all the fair,
   Bright, gentle sisterhood that blossom'd there
     In the home-garden; and thou gav'st it me,
With these sad words — "The last that I may see.
For when the glowing spring-time comes again,
And all the fields are rich with mellow grain,
And fair the roses which have crowned the May —
I may lie lowly, as they lie to-day;
The ice upon my heart, and form, and face;
The flowers waving o'er my resting-place."

Thou, mother, who hast seen the roses fall,
Whose hands have culled the fairest of them all,
To lay upon my table, there to bloom;
Whose sylph-like gliding in my lonely room,
Brightened into cheer the sombre gloom;
Thou, whose love, sweet, yet unlike the flowers,
Knows ne'er a fading, when the winter lowers.
Thou, whose blessed life of chastened grace
Shines through the holy beauty of thy face;
Whose watch was ceaseless through my darkling
    night;
Thou couldst not die, and take away the light
From me, thy stricken child! it cannot be.
Others have slept that pale sleep silently;
Some are more silent, who sleep not — to me:

Whose voiceless lives are harder far to bear,
Than though I knew them stilly resting there.

And, oh! will you too leave me, mother dear?
My soul is sick with agonizing fear.
Let the flowers fall, and the chill winds blow,
And on earth's countless treasures heap the snow;—
Let fire consume the dross, but not my gold;
The purchase-coin of joy ne'er bought or sold
With years and time. Oh! let me give to thee
All things else dear, who gave life to me.
But *do not leave* me, mother; when you go,
I too must wither while the chill winds blow,
For all life's roses will be hid with snow.
Better a grave with thee in yon sweet spot,
Than all the desert-world where thou art not.

SOMEWHERE.

THOU art dying, poor old year!
  And around thy snow-crowned bier,
  Spirits through the silent night,
Weave a shroud of meshes white.

On this pass of death and birth
Somewhere o'er the silent earth,
One is straying, who can know,
Life above, nor grave below.

In the matin-time somewhere,
Bows a heart in voiceless prayer.
May he come to rest at last,
Where we trysted in the past.

Where the ages, too, lie dumb,
Glacier-seal'd for the to-come.
Dead for time that they might be
Born to God's infinity.

GENIUS.

TO clothe life's chaos wild with beauteous grace,
And through lost Edens of the heart to trace
The soul's high majesty of recompense;
To lift the mind from out the slough of sense,
And climb the steeps of truth to palace fair
Of thought set on the hills of God; to bear
Time's burdens up with patient faith, and back
Through vales of storm to seek earth's hidden track:
This, Genius, is thy work — to wait and keep
Still watches while the Lord's beloved sleep.

To wander, homeless, through a world of homes;
To look with longing on earth's countless tombs
Which mark the way; with hunger of the soul
To yearn for rest with fever 'yond control
Drinking life's vital springs; in vain to cleave

With heart of worship to the forms that leave
Their clayey touch upon pure spirit-shrines;
To delve for gems of worth in sordid mines
Of coarse humanity; to trust in vain;
To love when love brings naught save endless pain:
To toil with laggard step and weary mien,
Through mazy darks of time, for light unseen;
To sow, but never reap; to weave a crown
From roses of the heart, and wander down
The ages crownless, though another wear
In hope the garlands won from thy despair;
To live alone in crowds; to die alone;
To faint and fall unwept — life's duty done:
This, Genius, is the doom fate metes thee here —
A life despoiled — a solitary bier —
A rack'd soul and brain — a starved frame;
And on the marble at thy head — a name!
Posterity thy heritage will claim at last,
When thou shalt sleep, forgotten with the past.

Favored of God — misunderstood of men —
To thy Creator clear 'yond mortal ken.
This for thyself: But what for world and man
Hast thou wrought blindly on life's little span
Of days?— a path of light through mazes cold
Mid Alpine fastness or in desert old;
Hast brought to mind of earnest hope one spring
Of which to quaff — new life inspir'd — to bring
Pilgrims athirst to the pure fount of truth —
Of which one drop to failing age or youth,

Given in faith, were given Him who gave
The soul's majestic power, life to save.

Many forget the singer, though the song
Still lingers, with sweet cadence borne along
The way, to soothe with whisperings of heaven.
They pass the teacher by, who purg'd the leaven
From their young minds; though his pure lessons still
May live to good, — words of wisdom will.

Though far from full the measure of thy days,
Christ's livery was suffering! thorny ways
Through earth, a cross, and death of shame and pain.
" Be that ye mete to others thine again;
And that which ye receive shall make you blest
In the bright vistas of infinite rest, —
The place prepared by Him who trod before
This strait of time to the great evermore."

TO BELLE F. C.

 HAVE missed you, darling, missed you,
In the twain of years which rung
Their wild wail of solemn cadence,
Down my heart's deep chords among.
In the amber-light of morning;
In the noon's broad, fervid glow,
In the golden slant of even;

In the darkness of my woe;
In the still, mysterious midnight!
When my heart was breaking slow,—
Breaking for your angel-presence;
For your kiss on lip and brow;
For your soft, white arms about me,—
Darling, and I miss you now.

I have loved you, darling, loved you!
With a love that knew no blight,
And a trust that knew no dimness
In the darkness of the night.
With a spirit leal to shield you;
With a longing for your touch;
With a grace that held you ever,
In the heart which suffered much.
Loved you with a hope though hopeless,
With a tenderness of ruth,
And a love that clung so truly,
With no recompense of truth.

I shall love you, darling, love you,
Till the years shall be no more;
Years through which our souls cry vainly
For the joys we knew before.
I shall miss you, darling, miss you,
Miss your face and your caress,
Till within time's distant Aidenn,
I shall find you and my rest.

When the days of earth are ended,
Days of longing, want, and care,

And my soul goes home at even,
Through the soft, ethereal air,
Up along the starry stairway
To a palace bright and fair,
I shall know that it is Heaven,
Darling, when I greet you there.

TO ———

CAN the fates say why they could not last,
The golden hours that have flown so fast
Since we two met in the recent past?

Was it just because they were so bright,
Time glided by like a fairy sprite,
Leaving no trace in his trackless flight?

But the tides must cease their airy flow;
We shall miss thy face's genial glow,
In our coming spring when the roses blow.

When the summer song-bird's notes are heard
And boundless deeps of soul are stirred
No longer by thy pleasant word.

When the solemn stars of winter gleam,
And the moon sends down her silver beam,
And day lies locked in silent dream;—

SONNET.

We 'll muse of thee through many an hour,
In the light of memory's magic power,
Till the year has passed from snow to flower.

It will come too soon — some early day —
The farewell clasp, the separate way,
And all that has been a memory.

Yet some little word of mine, I ween,
And the tear-drops falling all unseen,
Will keep that memory fresh and green.

And when God's eternal morn shall blend
With a noon of joy which has no end,
I will hail thee, then, my soul's true friend.

SONNET.

THERE is to-day a touch upon my heart!
A tone within so clear, which doth impart
Unto my weary soul the grace of rest,
My spirit, mother, seeks the parent nest:
Its wings are flagging in the outward reach
Of thought — far lying 'yond the range of speech;
All space is compassed by the shining beam
Of thy sweet love; and doth thy goodness seem,
More prized by me than richest treasure won
By mental toil, or noblest duty done.

O mother, dearest! take my loyal heart;
It is thine own, the purer, better part
Of what I have to give. On sacred shrine
Of love and home I lay it, mother mine!

"BINGEN ON THE RHINE."

T was a simple, uncouth, soiled print;
   A lithograph of ancient style — and bent
   Around a circling board so carelessly,
Damp with the drizzle of the humid day.
One poor old German, who had turned back
From his long gazing on the seaward track,
That snow-reefed passway to the *faderland*,
Paused, drew across his eyes a toil-worn hand;
Then bent them in a sad and rigid stare,
Upon the simple picture hanging there.

He car'd not though the tides should ebb and flow,
And busy boatmen to their homes did go,
E'en while the tramp of many thousand feet
Waxed faint and fainter in the twilight street.
Severed there from kith of humankind,
With many a sad thought rankling in his mind;
Swaying the poor old clay with mighty swell;
For *Bingen on the Rhine*, the tear-drops fell.

The tides surged slowly backward o'er the past,
To Bingen on the Rhine, as seen at last,
By this poor exile from his land afar,
Borne thence by poverty and luckless war,
To seek a clime of peace and work! — but now,
Crushed by life's sorry ills, he bent his brow,
And trembling like the rolling sea he crossed,
Again wept for the Bingen he had lost;
While the chill-blankness of a mute despair,
Closed with the hazy night around him there.

Anon, the lamps were lighted in the street!
A watchman slowly paced his lonely beat,
Until the steeple-clock told twelve — and then
The officer addressed him: "Ho! my friend,
'T is time you sought your quarters for the night."
How the touch startled him! — the old man's sight
Was surely failing; wife and children all,
Were clustered round him; the stranger's call,
Had rent again the dear, long-severed band,
Dispelled the dream of home and *faderland*.

Slowly he moved away; while each fell stroke,
Which echoed through the night, some fetter broke
That bound him to the happy past. Awhile
He toiled the days through, with a patient smile
Curving the poor, pale lips; God knew that he
Sought Bingen "*in the better counterie.*"

KINDRED GRAVES.

WINDS of autumn, touch them gently!
    Snows of winter, very lightly!
        Wrap those mounds afar,
Through the world in all her roaming —
Finds that friend in sorrow's gloaming,
        Nothing half so fair —
As the pure heart-blossoms faded,
When she left them meekly sleeping —
        Her loved ones there.

Spring's bright roses twice have blossom'd,
Since she saw upon her bosom —
        Bertie fade away;
When she laid him wildly weeping
In the chilly gloom of winter —
        On a solemn day.
Laid him gently with the rarest
Halo on his face's fairness
        In the frozen clay.

By a tomb where dewy showers
Gemmed the grass in summer hours,
        On the vale below;
Birds sang matins in the wildwood,
Orphan voices wept in childhood,
        For another woe:

KINDRED GRAVES.

While the solemn stars were sleeping,
Like the mother gone to heaven —
    Very long ago.

And a grave yet wider — deeper;
Of another silent sleeper —
    Resting all alone.
Ever brave and nothing fearing,
Turn'd to God for patient hearing,
    When the strife was done;
With a faith that never faltered
In the mad, victorious conflict —
    Till the end was won.

"Cannons' roar" and "muskets' rattle,"
"Or the din of distant battle,"
    Ne'er can reach him more.
Every sound of hoping, fearing,
Fainter grew as he was nearing
    The eternal shore!
Voice of mother, child, nor brother
Cometh like the sun to cheer her,
    Never any more.

REDEEMED BY LOVE.

MOTHER, come and sit beside me;
   Do not fear to touch me now,
   For the mocking phantoms leave me
When your hand is on my brow.
All the madness surging o'er me
   Quails before that look of thine,
And the flush of wine and fever
   Pales as moans the soughing wind.

Mother, all will soon be over!
   I am nearing yonder strand
Where your voice may not recall me,
   Nor the clinging of your hand.
Wasted years I have rehearsed —
   Reckless, squandered with a will —
Bought, this doom of the accursed,
   From the demon of the still.

But the time has come, dear mother —
   I have bartered life for this!
Hell is yawning! Press another
   On my lips — *just one, last kiss.*
It will still the serpent-hisses
   That are sounding in my soul.
Who could dream such things were lurking
   'Neath the sparkle of the bowl?

Clasp me in your arms, dear mother,
  From those glaring demons there.
Don't you see their eyeballs glitter
  Through the glamour of the air?
And upon the coming dawn-time
  There's a brand of lurid gloom —
Burning, flaming like the taper —
  Which will light me to the tomb.

Oh, I might have stayed beside you!
  Yet I left for fiends like these!
Would to God that I might keep you!
  You my only hope of peace.
I have been a blight upon you,
  And a scourge, for all your care.
Mother, oh! can you forgive me?
  It will lighten my despair.

I am going, mother. Kiss me,
  As you used to long ago,
Ere I changed your angel presence
  For the haunts of crime and woe; —
Though I ne'er forgot you, mother —
  Never, amid mirth or pain,
It was that which broke my fetters —
  Brought me to your side again.

Oh, I am so happy, mother!
  All my woe has changed to bliss,
Since I summon'd strength to see you —
  Strength of love to tell you this;

And have felt your arms about me —
　Your warm kiss on cheek and brow.
You have blessed me — God forgive me!
　Mother, I can leave you now.

Meekly, in the calm of morning,
　Low upon her bended knee,
Sank the mother — light adorning
　Her angelic brow.   And see,
Close beside him still she lingers,
　With the loved and erring dead,
Pressing yet the rigid fingers —
　Thinking of the words he said.

Thinking how upon her bosom,
　Years ago she blessed him there;
Then a little fairy prattler,
　Climbing on his mother's chair.
He had loved her, oh! how dearly!
　Was it strange she could not blame —
Only pity him, thus early
　Passed beyond his grief and shame?

Then she bent her eyes upon him!
　Glowing on the waxen face,
There she saw the Master's signet,
　Of his blest redeeming grace.
The same love which drew him to her,
　When the tempter pressed him sore,
Led him very near to heaven,
　Ne'er to wander any more.

Christ, the God of the transgressor!
  How her heart gave thanks to him,
Who had laid her idol shattered
  In the silence, cold and grim.
Though his life was lost in folly,
  Death had hidden in the bowl,
This one amulet of pardon,
  To redeem his wayward soul.

TO E. L. S.

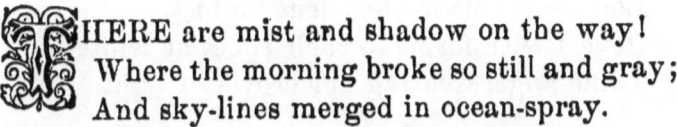HERE are mist and shadow on the way!
Where the morning broke so still and gray;
And sky-lines merged in ocean-spray.

And life-tides rolling dark and high;
Stifling the tones of thy sad heart-cry,
Hiding heaven from thy tearful eye.

Thy noontide joy has changed to gloom!
The world once filled with light and bloom,
Holds darkness and a mother's tomb.

We heard the chime of the boatman's oar,
Touching the sands on the golden shore,
With its lighthouse gleaming evermore.

On the bright track o'er which she passed,
When her frail earth-bark was strandward cast,
A steady glory streamed at last,

Over the snow of its pure white sails;
Fanned by breath of a thousand gales;
As the sinking sun o'er twilight trails.

Yet live this thought in thy heart so true,
Bowed o'er that grave where the sod is new,
While the cold stars glimmer faint and few:

And the spring-winds whisper, "she is gone!"
O friend of mine, grief-scourged and lone,
Though strong of soul in thy trial grown,

Let visions oft in the silent night,
Reveal with forms in their robes of white,
Thine angel wearing her crown of light.

THE BROWN HAND.

GENTLY it lies, like a crisp leaf,
    Upon my child's bright hair —
Protection from each clinging grief —
    A shield from every care.

Ah me! it seems a little while
    Since on her orphan-life
A cruel blow of blight and guile
    Beat cold and hard their strife —

THE BROWN HAND.

Upon her heart and mine, ere we
    From out the world's dark ways
Found refuge 'neath the old roof-tree,
    As in the childhood days.

Where, years agone, upon my head
    The same brown hand was prest,
That father-face bent o'er my bed —
    Soothed then his child to rest —

Now cradles mine with tender name —
    Love in his soft brown eyes.
No time can ever dim the flame
    Where home-peace, brooding, lies.

Oh! with that dear toil-brown'd hand
    To guide us and to bless,
Through sun-bright ways to God's far land,
    We 're borne by his caress:

And should the brown hand palsied lie —
    The words from his dear lips
E'er cease to flow — the gentle eye
    Grow dark in death's eclipse, —

We pray that strength to bear the blow
    Would unto us be given,
And faith to seek through life's drear woe
    Our father dear in heaven.

JUSTICE.

A SONNET.

THOU potent spirit of the good and true,
    Thine is no craven, coward heart of fear;
Thine no blanch'd face or soul where falsehood
    grew,
    To smirk at truth, and traitor-shape to wear.
Thy hand will not fan envy's secret fires;
    Thy heart will hold no malice, strife, or hate,
Nor lips will echo back the scourge of liars,
    Or ready brain for time's defences wait;
Nor with thy silence prate when hope expires,
    When one small word might turn the scale of fate.
Thine is no voice to lead astray the blind,
    Or deal the husks of swine to striving worth.
Thine is a soul of ruth for human-kind —
    A lever by which man may move the earth.

TO MY FRIEND,

C. D. P., OF WASHINGTON, D. C.

THERE'S a spirit most divine
In the manliness of thine,
And a goodness pure and true
Where thy soul its blossoms grew; —
Recompense of word and deed,
Toward humanity the meed
Of thy charity awarding; —
Every toil and pain recording,
In the pity of thy heart,
Feeling of their wrongs a part,
And a wish to bear their burden
To yon still, far-lying guerdon,
O'er the deserts of the way,
To the dawn of calmer day,
When life's warfare shall be ended,
Purpose and fulfilment blended.

Oh! if words and wishes brought
E'er for thee the boon I sought,
Then life's fate would ne'er dissever,
E'er for thee or thine forever,
One bright link in all the chain
Of thy heart-life, — woe nor pain
With their blighting force descend
On the path of wife or friend.

Joy be thine in years to come,
Here or in thy future home —
When the shadows of time's even
Melt into the light of heaven.

"NEVER AGAIN."

THOSE dirge-like words to the slow heart-beat
Of years ring out! and the sunder'd chain
Which bound his life in its far retreat,
Circles our souls with a wordless pain
And shuddering chill. Ah me! to greet
The far-off dead in his winding-sheet,
  "Never again."

In a hallow'd place, so still and cold,
They made thy grave in the frozen mould:
With rigid hands that were idle near,
While he could work for his dear ones here,
Over the passionless bosom pressed;
They left him there, in his dreamless rest;
In the boundless spring which blooms afar,
Where the nights of death their glory mar —
  "Never again."

Never again will the broken band,
Be reunited until we stand
With those we love in the better land,
Round the great white throne! What joy to greet
Them yonder — whom in this world we'll meet —
  "Never again."

THE TABLET.

A LITTLE tablet pure and white,
To mark a day so sweetly bright,
With sunshine of a by-gone time;
Whose summers, with their golden chime,
Rung through its mystic-winged hours;
Fraught with perfumes of rich flowers,
And music rare of human tones —
Whose spell my soul in secret owns:
And kindly words that long will dwell
Within my being's inmost cell.
The earnest clasp of severed hands;
A linking firm of golden bands —
To form a chain of wondrous grace,
With which to circle time and space.
A breathing of some treasured things!
The compensation friendship brings;
Whose soul is truth and honor blent,—
Whose life was from the Father sent.

It is of these my tablet tells,
Sweet tones like memory's silver bells —
Chime through the silence of my heart;
Their melody will ne'er depart.
And charmed by the sweet refrain,
I plant it on earth's brightest plain;
To lift its spire to heaven, and be
An "*in memoriam*" of thee.

"SUMMER GONE."

IN MEMORY OF MRS. H. A. W.

WHEN last summer's skies were fair,
   And its roses blooming bright,
  Fell sweet incense-laden air,
   Morning gleams of Eden light,
Round her form a joyous bride;
   Trusting whom her love had won.
Winter came! orange-flowers
   Faded in the "summer gone."

In the clammy, frozen clay,
   Stranger hands have made her tomb;
Chill winds mournfully to-day
   Chant a dirge for blighted bloom —
Broken hopes: — a stricken form
   Walks a life-path sad and lone,
Through its tempest and its storm,
   Dreaming of his "summer gone."

Oh, the chill and sunless day!
   Summer-wreaths lie faded now:
She is sleeping, blighted May,
   With a chaplet on her brow.
Joy's bright way is steeped with tears.
   Crossing o'er the night to morn!
In God's record of our years
   We shall find the "summer gone."

"JOHN HALIFAX, GENTLEMAN."

A LAD of humble birth, and poor was he,
With soul of loftier nobility
Than kings and princes boast! A gentleman,
Whose noble pride made e'er his bearing grand.
He loved *a lady* who had mines of gold,
A spirit high, a form of lovely mould.
Almost divine, and madly worshipped so,
Could not give back his jewels-like? oh, no!
She was so beauteous, too, he could not dare
To hope that she would listen to his prayer,
Or come to love the humble tanner's lad,
In station far below; yet she was glad
To have the strong man for her friend when he
And she, and death, were guests at Enderly.
Her heart looked up to him that bitter hour,
As to a strong, strong stay whose potent power
Was all-sufficient.
    Soon, the parting o'er;
Cruel it was — he saw the social door
Closed by the hand of wealth and power,
And cursed his destiny that bitter hour.
With strange intent upon his face so wan,
He rose him up, a hopeless, broken man,
All faint and heart-sore like a homeless child.
The burning fever in his veins grew wild,
Sapping life's current from his athlete frame,

While striving for the rest which never came;
Resolved to go away across the sea,
And try to bear his burden patiently;
To seek a respite which he could not find,
From the great grief which preyed upon his mind.

Phineas sought Ursula, with the bold intent,
To tell her he should go, and *why* he went.
He found her sitting with the sunbeams round
Wrapped in their golden tissue. As the sound
Of his impatient feet broke on the day,
She, rising, blushed, scarce knowing what to say —
When, with a faltering tongue, outspoke the friend —
To her whom " David loved!" yet who could send
Him by her coldness all that gloomy way,
Without one look or tone to bid him stay.

Away went Phineas; for he feared the smart
Of her apparent coldness. Woman's heart!
What worldless man can read? When he was gone,
She sat, the fair head bowed her hands upon;
Then she rose up, and found a swift, sure way
To his dear side. The woman in her spoke
Strong words that cleft the ice! each daring stroke
Some vestige of the faded fetters broke.

"And you did love him?" said his friend, in glee.
"John knows," she answered him, "and *he will stay.*"
And there was given them a life-long love,
Of usefulness on earth — and rest above.

"MY YEARS GO ON."

TINY span they seem — not many gone.
    A merry child, to whom the world was new,
  I made my playhouse on yon sloping lawn,—
    The sward my carpet, — 'neath the blighted yew.
The place has lost its fresh, bright look of yore;
    The old yew shivers in the wind; anon
A blight will grow upon the glory wore
    By these mute faces as "my years go on."

I'm thinking of the broken household-band —
    The three remaining, and the one asleep,
The faded daisies and the falling sand,
    The patient, willing eyes love-taught to weep;
The mansion in my heart with shapes of trust:
    All, as the morning radiant; one by one
They crumbled! Now, alas! the clinging dust
    Lies on their fairness, though "my years go on."

While I a wanderer o'er the earth's broad track —
    Lonely amid these early scenes — yet stay,
As some weird pilgrim who has turned back
    From the cold mazes of a weary way,
Feeling within my heart a hungry pain —
    A longing never still beneath the sun, —
I try to rest me in the shade again,
    Yet only shiver "while my years go on."

"MY YEARS GO ON."

Ah me! a far, blue track appears again, —
    A long way off it seems, this dreary day.
Memory thrills me with a touch of pain,
    The landmarks are so changed along life's way.
Once more they greet me — the bright shapes and fair,
    Whose destiny was heaven early won.
For them the spring no pallid masks can wear, —
    No worn, white faces as "my years go on."

A hallowed brightness o'er pale beauty cast —
    A shining peace upon each waiting face,
As of tired wanderers safe at last —
    At rest within the fold, through Jesus' grace.
It was so hard to give them up! — to roam
    The life-way, missing them! — stricken alone
To thread the spaces in my heart, and come
    To do without them as "my years go on!"

Yet, oh! in days to come, when ages bow
    Before the great I Am of future time, —
Who wears the morning's signet on his brow,
    And holds the destinies of every clime, —
I will not count life by this little span —
    These wasted hopes and dreams that leave me lone;
For broken shapes of earth stand clear and grand
    In the forever, as God's " years go on."

ROSA.

GIRLHOOD with its mazy pleasure
    Shrouds thee now.
There's a glory-passing measure
    On thy brow;
And thy heart enshrineth treasure,
    Pure, I trow, —

As the radiance gleaming ever
    O'er life's morn;
Barred as by hope's golden lever,
    To adorn
Earth with light of the forever
    Heaven-born.

Time is wide — its ways are weary!
    May thy feet
Safely cross its deserts dreary:
    Thy heart beat,
To life's solemn cadence — cheery
    Music sweet.

With its halo resting lightly
    On thy brow,
To thy love-star shining brightly
    Lowly bow,
Asking God to keep thee — nightly,
    Pure as now.

"SHADOWED LIGHT."

THERE are words that burn deep on the barrenest brain;
There are torches aflame on love's altars of pain;
There are tones like the chant of the stars at their birth;
There are faces like light 'mid the chaos of earth;
There are matins of morn and vespers of even —
Confusing the world with the splendor of heaven.

There are links frail as withes of the glittering sand;
There are vows "writ in water," and wrecks on the land;
There are storms 'neath the calms of the cavernous deeps —
In limitless darks where the sea-coral sleeps;
There are souls that *must sing* and hearts that will cling —
Though death be the portion their loyalty bring.

One short year agone, when the season was new —
Bright May 'neath the sky and the sun in its blue,
And flowers lifted up their pale lips in the noon,
Borne down by the breath of the desert simoon,
While drinking the crystal whose roseate rise
Was quenched by the flame in his luminous eyes.

"SHADOWED LIGHT."

Yet he kissed the white petals with passionate lips,
Till their fragrance was by his great glory eclipsed;
Then left them to die in the glare of the day,
Where the wind and the wave at their work seem'd to play,
While darkness came down, and the pitiless sun,
Who cared not to keep what his luminance won,
Went back to his course through the anemone blue,
As if love were a falsehood, and God were not true.

Now I sit in the glow of the Protean spring!
My thoughts flitting gayly as birds on the wing,
And my heart with the past and the present at play,
With flowers at the feet of the laureate May.
A glory comes o'er me — the sun of my dream,
With eyes like his splendor and soul like his beam;
While the earth and the sea, and the heaven above,
All glow with the dream of immaculate love.

But the vision goes out! and I pray while I weep
For the quiet and peace of that passionless sleep,
'Neath flowers on the plains of summers to be
In the emerald reach of eternity —
Where the "light in the dust" will never lie dead,
Though *I rest* with a stone at my feet and my head.

AUGUSTINE.

NO more, oblivious of time or place,
 To hoard a waiting blessing on thy lips:
But cross thy heart, above a loved face,
 And bow thine head as 'neath the sun's eclipse!
To wait the morning-light, and seek to trace
 Christ in the dumb pain thy trial has been.
A strange and wayward destiny is thine,
 A mystery sad, of anguish, Augustine.

Men look upon thy face so stern and pale,
 Nor see beneath thy proud and careless mien —
A life despoiled for aye, nor catch thy wail
 Of spirit o'er wrecked worlds! The sunset sheen
Upon death's gathering ice, the whited sail
 Adrift like snow-flake on a sea of green,
And clinging myrtle over graves a trail,
 Are as thy broken love-dream, Augustine.

Crushed May-time flowers on life's autumn beat,
 Of duty's sentry-guard o'er soul of man, —
'Mid lingering fragrance of pale roses sweet,
 Left far behind thee in the shrivelled span —
Thy years have grown to be: no more to meet
 That soul's reproachful gaze beneath the ban
And curse that withers thee. *Time is too fleet*
 In which to live thy soul's life, Augustine.

AUGUSTINE.

A glorious life of rapture, which was planned
  Where tropic skies bend low, and azure seas
Amoaning kiss a fair Provencian strand,
  And Eden fragrance fills the summer breeze.
Oh! wreck of wasted strength and ruin grand,
  And desolating scourge of templed ease,
And world's dread minion, care, whose mighty hand
  Hast broken altars of thy spirit, Augustine.

The soil of mind, when pure, great fruits may grow!
  Though not on plains where dead-sea deserts lie:—
On which thy palsied heart is stricken low,
  Beneath the glacier-gleam of life gone by.
Behold thine autumn in its sombre glow,
  Grow pale with winter in the sunset sheen!
Of Memory's *crown* upon a brow of snow:
  And speak a long, long farewell, Augustine.

Life's sacrificial draughts the spirit purge,
  And dead-sea fruits enrich the deathless soul.
Above thy years let blood-stained billows surge,
  Till spirit-robes are white and life made whole;
The life whose clinging curse and final scourge
  Was man's "*too late*" upon death's open scroll.

. . . .

The soul's eternal loves immutable are thine,
  God and his everlasting ages, Augustine.

THE LOVED AND LOST.

OVER the bridge which the angels crost,
   And up through the shining gates of pearl,
    Pass'd the souls of our loved and lost
Through crystal doors of the silent world.

High in heaven, where the angels chant
   Sweet songs of love to the Saviour-king,
Mingling their notes with those who went
   To join the saints in their worshipping.

Foster and *Freddie* are 'mid the throng,
   With radiant brows and robes of white,
The brightest spirits of earth among
   The children-choir in the realm of light.

FINALE.

HROUGH fate's night so cold and dark —
Two souls drifting from God's arc —

Over separate waves were borne,
In the dimness of the morn.

'Neath the noon's broad, glowing sun,
Two were mingled into one.

. . . .
. . . .

In the golden slant of even —
Came the twain, one soul, to Heaven.

www.ingramcontent.com/pod-product-compliance
Lightning Source LLC
Chambersburg PA
CBHW030311170426
43202CB00009B/957